THE FUTURE AND LOCAL GOVERNMENT

THE COLLABORATIVE COUNCIL

A STUDY OF INTER-AGENCY WORKING IN PRACTICE

Robin Hambleton, Sue Essex,
Liz Mills and Konica Razzaque

ISBN 0 904677 72 9
LGC Communications 1995
33-39 Bowling Green Lane, London EC1R ODA
Telephone 0171 837 1212 Fax 0171 837 2725
Printed by Black Bear Press

i

Acknowledgements

The authors wish to thank the Joseph Rowntree Foundation for its funding and support for this study. A large number of people have helped us during the course of this research project. First of all, we would like to thank Tony Cross who was an original member of the research team. He helped to formulate the research proposal and carried out much of the work on the transport case study before leaving the university to take up a post as chief public transport planner with West Sussex CC in January. Second, we are indebted to the respondents in the various authorities and agencies who gave time to be interviewed. Their understanding and comments provide the essential case study material for this project.

We were greatly assisted by a project advisory group which met regularly during the course of the project and gave invaluable advice and guidance. We are most grateful for the time and help the group gave. The members of this group were:

Pat Kneen (Chair), Senior Research Officer, Joseph Rowntree Foundation
Alan Barnish, Chief Executive, Shropshire CC
Gareth Wyn Jones, Professor, and formerly Director of Science and Policy Development, Countryside Council for Wales
Joan Jones, Deputy Secretary, Association of Metropolitan Authorities
Peter Slater, Secretary of the Standing Conference on Regional Policy in South Wales
Murray Stewart, Professor, School for Advanced Urban Studies, University of Bristol
Tony Travers, Director of Research, Greater London Group, London School of Economics

This final report is, however, the responsibility of the research team.

Finally, we would like to offer a special thankyou to the secretaries in the Department of City and Regional Planning and, in particular, to Cynthia Trevett who, as well as producing this finished document, has provided support to various members of the research team throughout the research project.

Robin Hambleton, Sue Essex, Liz Mills and Konica Razzaque
Department of City and Regional Planning,
University of Wales College of Cardiff,
PO Box 906,
Cardiff CF1 3YN.

August 1995

Contents

1. Introduction

For a variety of reasons local authorities are becoming less inward looking and are developing diverse ways of working with other agencies. The reasons why councils are branching out are examined further below. At the outset, however, we can note that the traditional, monolithic model of local government, the model which sees local authorities as institutions concerned simply to collect taxes and deliver services, is not well suited to the challenges now facing them. Changes in both the policy environment and the institutional environment are spurring local authorities to shift their focus from an exclusive concern with the direct provision of a range of services towards ways of working which involve the creation of partnerships with other authorities and agencies.

In some areas of policy making the importance of inter-agency working is well established. Strategic land-use planning and integrated transport planning are just two areas of policy making where the importance of developing effective collaboration between local authorities and other agencies has been mainstream practice for more than 20 years. In recent years, however, it has been recognised that a growing number of emerging, multi-faceted problems cry out for co-ordinated and well ordered responses. In areas as diverse as urban regeneration,[1] community care[2] and environmental policy,[3] local authorities are now urged to work more closely and effectively, not just with other levels of government, but also with other arms of government, with the voluntary sector and with the private sector.

The fragmentation of local government

At the same time as changes in the policy environment point towards the need for improvements in inter-agency working, the institutional environment within which local authorities must operate has become more fragmented. New local institutions have been created, such as training and enterprise councils (TECs) and urban development corporations (UDCs), while old institutions have become fragmented, such as in the separation of purchasing and providing roles in the health service and numerous local government services. The co-organisers of a recent Joseph Rowntree Foundation seminar on local governance concluded:

> "There is richness in this fragmentation but there are weaknesses as well. The interplay of organisations and interests can better reflect the realities of life; and the existence of organisations (and contracts) with specific objectives can produce more effective service delivery. However, there is no guarantee of a strategic framework within which all can operate and direct their energies and attention, there are weaknesses in accountability and

1

there is often a yawning gap between those involved in governance and the governed."[4]

The local authority stands in the middle of all these changes as the only elected body with the political legitimacy to take a broad view. In some ways these changes represent a threat to local government — certainly functions have been taken away. However, it can also be argued that they provide new opportunities for local authorities to develop productive relationships with other organisations. In any event, it seems clear that the effective local authority of the future will need to be imaginative in its approach to inter-agency working. This publication is a contribution, based on case study research, to the development of ideas on how to improve inter-organisational working at local level.

Legislative, financial, political and social changes are transforming the nature of local government. In many ways the trend has been towards a diversification of the agencies delivering local services. The following illustrations support this point:

● The transfer of functions from local authorities to other agencies — for example, housing associations

● The creation of agency agreements to manage specialised functions — for example, economic development and business advice services

● The introduction of compulsory competitive tendering (CCT) which has heightened the role of private agencies and arm's length direct labour organisations in providing services

● The decentralisation of power to local service delivery units (for example, schools) or other bodies (for example, residents' groups).

In other ways current shifts may lead to a bringing together of separate institutions. Certainly the reorganisation of local government in Wales, Scotland and parts of England is intended to unify the services presently provided by the district and county tiers of local government. These changes, however, will not remove the need for the new unitary councils to collaborate on issues and concerns which straddle their boundaries. Also, in more than a few areas of England there will be hybrid structural arrangements — that is, areas where new unitaries will be created within areas which will continue to be two tier. In such areas, effective inter-authority collaboration will be very important if public services are to be managed effectively. Likewise, in the areas not directly affected by structural change many councils now recognise that new ways of improving joint working between the tiers of local government need to be developed.

From local government to local governance

In addition to the changes imposed by legislation and the structural reshaping of local government, it is possible to detect wider forces which are leading local authorities to redefine their roles and relationships. Many local authorities are questioning long-established organisational assumptions and are beginning to recognise that, while direct provision may often continue to be the best strategy for meeting local needs, there can be significant advantages in working with and through other agencies.

Some councils have, however, resisted the idea of developing an "enabling role" for local government as they have associated such an approach with the views of a Conservative government. In the late 1980s and early 1990s many local authorities objected to the idea of enabling, as they viewed it as a form of rhetoric designed to mask a reduction in the direct power of local authorities. Enabling does not, however, require the dismantling of the local authority. It is crucial to consider who is being enabled to do what and to ask whose interests are being served. Some authorities put the emphasis on enabling local people to define and meet their own objectives. Others stress the importance of enabling the voluntary sector to be more effective. Yet others stress the importance of developing new kinds of partnership with the private sector. Depending on the ends pursued, enabling could lead to an expanding role for the local authority.

There is an ongoing and lively debate in the UK around the theme "reinventing government".[5] A key theme is that governments, both central and local, should concentrate on "steering rather than rowing". On this analysis, too much of a focus on delivering services (rowing) can distract politicians from their key task of governing (steering). There is evidence that by forming partnerships or working agreements with outside agencies, local government can still achieve its objectives. The recent Local Government Management Board publication, *Working across organisational boundaries: learning from the Welsh experience*,[6] looked at some examples in Wales where an innovative approach to joint working had allowed common objectives to be achieved. Chwarae Teg (Fair Play) is such an example, where local government, local TECs, the Welsh Development Agency and private-sector organisations came together to fund a new organisation to achieve a common objective of helping women returners to work.

It is possible to summarise the arguments set out above by suggesting that we are witnessing a shift from local government to local governance. Such a shift was recognised in national advice on the future organisation and management of local government, *Fitness for purpose*. This report outlined the new challenges facing local government and suggested that any individual local authority can choose whether or not to concern itself with the wide range of problems and issues in its area:

> "Such an authority might identify a comprehensive range of local needs, prioritise them and use whatever means are appropriate to meet these needs. These could include direct or contracted-out service provision, inspection and regulation, and channels of influence and advocacy."[7]

Even an authority which places less emphasis on local governance cannot concentrate solely on the provision of its own services. Legislation, if nothing else, requires it to collaborate with other agencies in some areas of policy — for example, in relation to community care.

A key point which emerges from this discussion is that inter-agency working appears to be moving from the margins of local authority activity towards a more central position. Given the changes that have been outlined, it is important to study current experience with inter-agency working in practice in order to enhance understanding about the strengths and weaknesses of differing approaches.

This report

There are many reasons for developing inter-agency working. A recent Joseph Rowntree Foundation study examined the joint arrangements set up in Greater London and the metropolitan counties following the abolition of the county level of government in these areas in 1986.[8] It distinguished three main categories:

- Joint boards, which are required by law and have considerable independence, including powers to precept on district/borough councils for resources

- Joint committees, which are voluntarily created — though some may be virtually compulsory — which set a levy on the districts/boroughs and which may have their own officers and administrative structure or may rely on officers from constituent districts or boroughs

- Agency arrangements, where one district or borough provides a service on behalf of one or more other authorities.

The study of metropolitan experience concentrates on formal inter-authority mechanisms relating to functions and services required by statute.

This new report from the foundation is designed to complement the first study by primarily examining experience in non-metropolitan areas, by studying informal as well as formal mechanisms for collaboration, and by including voluntary and private-sector organisations as well as public bodies within the research. The overall aims of the study are:

1. To identify trends in the environment of local authorities which affect the need to work on a collaborative basis

2. To develop criteria for evaluating inter-agency working

3. To examine, through working examples, alternative ways of handling inter-agency policy making and management

4. To stimulate debate within local authorities about the importance of developing effective inter-agency arrangements.

The structure of this report reflects the three main phases of the research. Chapter 2 outlines the approach to evaluation — the criteria developed to assess inter-agency working, the selection of case studies and the way the research was carried out.

Four areas were chosen for study in order to encompass different inter-agency mechanisms in different policy settings.

The next four chapters discuss the arrangements for inter-agency collaboration in the four selected policy areas:

● Community care — involving joint planning between local authorities, health authorities, voluntary bodies and others to meet the needs of people with learning difficulties (Chapter 3)

● Strategic planning — involving informal collaboration between local authorities and central government agencies at a sub-regional or regional level (Chapter 4)

● Environmental policy — involving inter-agency collaboration between local authorities, voluntary bodies and others to pursue "greening" initiatives at local level (Chapter 5)

● Transport planning — involving the preparation of integrated transport strategies by groups of agencies at a local and sub-regional level (Chapter 6).

In order to generate fresh insights, all four case studies compare areas in Wales with areas in England.

Chapter 7 provides a commentary on the main themes revealed to be significant during the research:

- The role of central government
- The role of regional government
- The role of local government
- The role of non-governmental organisations
- The role of the private sector
- The role of the public
- The architecture of joint working
- The influence of resources
- Managing cultural realignment
- Identification and ownership
- Innovation.

The findings draw not only on documentary research but also on interviews with 61 actors currently involved in inter-agency collaboration.

Chapter 8 provides a summary of the main findings of the study and offers pointers for future policy.

2. Collaboration in context

The previous section outlined the reasons why inter-agency collaboration appears to be on the increase. In most, if not all, local authorities the idea of working with other organisations is increasingly accepted as a good thing. But this does not mean the practice of inter-agency collaboration receives unstinting support. On the contrary, there are substantial barriers to co-ordination. In the field of social policy these have been identified as vested interests, structural complexity and divergent professional and organisational cultures.[9] Taken to its extreme, this strand of argument amounts to a warning to invest as little time and as few hopes as possible in arrangements which require inter-agency collaboration.

It is important, then, to be clear about the obstacles facing those who are keen to improve inter-agency collaboration. Recent advice from the Local Government Management Board is well placed:

> "Powerful forces militate against the success of inter-agency working. Constant change within individual organisations and in the organisational landscape as a whole makes it difficult to build and sustain relationships. For instance, local authority managers find it hard to keep abreast of changes within health authorities. An emphasis on competition between agencies and on short-term measures of performance discourages the investment of time and knowledge required to develop joint working.

> "Financial cuts and the need to ration services ever-more stringently creates distrust between organisations and their clientele, and between different groups in society. As one hard-pressed institution withdraws from a particular area of service provision, another is left to pick up the pieces. As one agency has its budget cut, monies pass to a new body. Employees may have to be made redundant to maintain service levels, creating distrust between providers and consumers, and among staff. Such an atmosphere is antagonistic to inter-agency working that requires co-operation and trust."[10]

These barriers to co-ordination have led to some rethinking of the ideas which might underpin alternative approaches to co-ordination and joint working.

Alternative routes to effective co-ordination

Drawing on other recent research, we can suggest the problem of co-ordinating complex social and economic activities can be addressed in three different ways: hierarchy, markets and networks.[11] Each approach emphasises a different driving force. Hierarchy works through a chain of command. Market models achieve co-ordination through price signals which bring together demand and supply. Networks create a shared outlook which allows the pooling of resources to achieve a common purpose. It is worth examining each of these concepts in slightly more depth as they help to set the scene for the subsequent discussion.

Hierarchical relationships

Co-ordination within a single organisation can, to some extent, be enforced by hierarchical authority. For example, the chief executive of a local authority can require two departments to focus on a shared problem and bring forward proposals for change. Similarly co-ordination **between** organisations may be mandated by a third party. For example, central government can insist on the creation of a joint board to execute certain functions. A council with a clear hierarchy could allow a few people to represent the council with other agencies — it would be able to give them authority and then hold them to account.

Market relationships

In the 1980s, central government reacted against the idea of a planned and co-ordinated approach to public policy making. Instead the emphasis was placed on market models which, it was argued, would increase efficiency and strengthen accountability to consumers. Contracting arrangements between units (both within authorities and between authorities) would handle the problems of co-ordination. This model seems to be more easily achievable for services and activities which are relatively discrete. One problem with the market model is that it has not always proved possible to establish surrogates in the public sector which parallel the market dynamics of the private sector.

Network relationships

Networks are usually held together by shared beliefs and values rather than by contractual agreements. Networks are often thought of as flat organisational forms in contrast to the vertically organised hierarchy. They tend to be more open-ended and place more emphasis on trust and reciprocity. Network relationships imply informal relationships between essentially equal organisations and agencies. On the one hand, they allow for flexibility, can encourage innovation and can be used as vehicles for advocating new policies. However, it is the very informality of networks that gives rise to a certain amount of concern about how they work:

> "Co-ordination in this case may be settled in a less than open manner and not subject to any obvious accountability. A lot of networks are highly exclusive of outsiders."[12]

Much inter-agency working involves networking and the opening up of new communication channels cutting across lines of formal responsibility. It also implies the development of new skills and, in certain situations, the creation of new boundary spanning posts, sometimes referred to as reticulist or network roles.[13]

For the reasons outlined in Chapter 1, network relationships are becoming increasingly important. It would be a mistake to believe inter-agency working falls neatly within the third category of networking. Some forms of inter-agency working involve the exercise of hierarchical authority (for example, joint boards) while others involve various kinds of contracting (for example, agency arrangements). It is helpful, therefore, to recognise that different kinds of inter-agency arrangement engage the interest and enthusiasm of participants through different means. Any particular arrangement may be a hybrid in the sense that it may be sustained by more than one driving force.

Criteria for measuring inter-agency working

One aim of the research is to develop criteria for assessing inter-agency collaboration. A recent study of joint working in metropolitan areas suggested that successful joint action requires two components — **effective delivery** of function and adequate **accountability**. The overarching requirements of effectiveness and accountability may be in tension:

> "If strong accountability is the objective then voluntary arrangements are likely to be preferred. This option provides for the greatest degree of local input and control . . . Conversely, if the primary aim is the discharge of the function then statutory arrangements may be the only way of securing effective provision."[14]

It is a simplification but, for inter-agency arrangements driven by hierarchical relationships, there appears to be a choice. Are participants answerable only to their parent bodies? If yes, then from the point of view of those bodies, the accountability controls remain strong. However, a potential drawback with voluntary collaboration of this kind is that participants can remain disengaged. Unable to commit their organisations, participants can end up turning joint working into a talking shop rather than an arena for policy making and decision taking. This, the argument goes, undermines effectiveness.

In joint working there is, then, a potential tension between effectiveness and accountability. Much, however, depends on what the inter-agency collaboration is designed to achieve. In this research we have found it helpful to break down the broad categories of effectiveness and accountability into more specific criteria.

Effectiveness

This criterion concentrates on whether or not the arrangement is meeting its stated objectives. Where inter-agency arrangements seek to build partnerships between different organisations and interests, it is important that participants agree areas of common ground, identify shared goals and work to establish mutual respect, understanding and trust. This is not always easy as different actors often bring very different perspectives and demands to the negotiating table.

Within the effectiveness heading it is useful to distinguish the following criteria:

1. *Objectives.* What are the reasons for having the inter-agency arrangement? For example, it is important to distinguish between arrangements that:

- Make policy
- Influence policy
- Make decisions about the use of public resources
- Focus on a practical outcome or implement a project
- Share information and experience.

2. *Value for money.* Does the expenditure of effort and resources on inter-agency collaboration represent good value for money? This may be difficult to assess but in an era of resource constraints it is crucial to avoid wasting time and effort.

3. *Responsiveness.* How responsive are the joint arrangements to the needs of different participants? In the past some joint arrangements have been set up and implemented in a very rigid form and this rigidity has increased over time. In these circumstances joint planning and decision making can become a kind of ritual dance which does little to improve the responsiveness of the various organisations and interests to changing needs. Clearly, joint working needs to avoid this trap.

4. *Stability and flexibility.* How resilient are the arrangements in the face of changing circumstances? The survival of joint arrangements depends partly on the support they enjoy from the participating agencies but also on the degree to which they can take on new challenges and seize new opportunities.

Accountability

Issues of accountability and democracy have come very much to the fore in recent months, partly due to debates on local government reorganisation, but also due to the work of the Commission for Local Democracy.[15] Set in the framework of local representative democracy, one of the frequent criticisms of joint working is that it can dilute, obscure and sometimes erase the process of accountability. Leach, for example, suggests that joint arrangements weaken the operation of unitary government and undermine accountability and comprehensibility.[16] Certainly joint arrangements raise important issues of accountability, particularly at a time when the accountability of non-elected bodies has become such a cause for concern.

Within the accountability heading it is useful to distinguish the following criteria:

1. *Relating to the public.* How can citizens hold those engaged in inter-agency collaboration to account? A concern here is that the public may not only be unclear about where responsibility lies but may also find it difficult to get their views represented within the inter-agency arrangement. In considering this criterion we have found it helpful to distinguish the public at large from the interested public. It may be that, in certain areas, the latter should be the focus of attention, rather than the former — for example, users and carers in relation to services for people with learning disabilities. This criterion raises questions about public transparency and public access to the inter-agency arrangement

2. *Political accountability.* How do elected politicians hold those engaged in inter-agency collaboration to account? Some areas of inter-agency working may not have a high political salience and it may not be necessary to have joint political machinery — for example, areas of technical collaboration. Others may have significant political implications and will require strong political involvement. An Association of District Councils' paper drew this distinction and suggested that, broadly speaking, those activities requiring joint action because of their specialist nature would be less likely to have political salience than those requiring joint action because of their territorial nature.[17] In any event, important questions are raised about the role of elected councillors and the degree to which inter-agency working is under the control of politicians.

3. *Financial accountability.* In inter-agency arrangements where decisions on spending are made, how is financial accountability maintained? Current debates about probity and accountability in public life suggest this is an issue which warrants attention.

This may not be a comprehensive list of criteria and, as the research unfolded, other issues emerged as significant. For example, the degree to which participants identify with a given inter-agency arrangement can affect its performance considerably. The criteria we have listed do, however, provide a valuable organising framework and may, in themselves, be useful to authorities and organisations wishing to review their own approach to inter-agency working.

Selection of case studies

To investigate the issues set out above, four topics were chosen as case studies. These were selected to illustrate a range of collaborative models (from formal through to very informal), a range of levels of decision making (from sub-regional strategy to specific projects in particular cities) and a range of policy areas (from land-use planning to social care). The research team was guided in the selection of the case studies by a project advisory group comprising practitioners and researchers involved with local government. This helped the team identify policy areas which would be of particular interest to policy makers and managers.

The four topic case studies are:

1. *Community care.* This combines local authorities, health authorities, voluntary bodies, users and carers in the planning and management of services for various care groups. In this study the focus is on people with learning difficulties.

2. *Strategic planning.* This involves the creation of standing conferences bringing local authorities together on a sub-regional or regional basis to develop strategic land use and associated policies.

3. *Corporate environmental policy and action.* This is concerned with the creation of new networks to address environmental issues and foster environmental projects at the local level.

4. *Transport planning.* This brings together counties, districts and other agencies to prepare integrated transport strategies and spending plans.

In each case study the approach to inter-agency working in more than one geographical area has been studied. All the case studies compare a geographical area in Wales with an area in England. This was designed to uncover whether there were differences in approach in English and Welsh authorities. In practice there are some interesting differences between, for example, the role of the English Government Office for the Regions and the Welsh Office. Mindful of the impending impact of local government reorganisation, the case studies have also been selected from areas that will be affected by structural change in the relatively near future. Both Wales and parts of south west England (notably Avon County) are affected by these changes in 1996. The transport case study extends further afield to include an examination of the West Midlands "package approach" to inter-agency working. This was included as it has a reputation for being an effective approach to inter-agency working.

Research method and general observations

The research method involved documentary research on each of the four policy areas to uncover the history and evolution of inter-agency working in each case. The evaluation work in the selected geographical areas was carried out through face-to-face interviews using a detailed questionnaire. We were concerned to interview a range of actors in each inter-agency network. **Table 1** sets out the organisational background of the people we interviewed. In Chapter 1 it was suggested that we are witnessing a shift from local government to local governance. **Table 1** lends support to this claim. While 54% of our respondents were from local authorities the remainder were from other agencies. In all cases it seems that local authorities are playing a significant and usually a leading role. However, these authorities are clearly not working in isolation. Rather the case studies provide a vivid picture of the **collaborative council** in action.

Table 1. Survey respondents by organisation

Organisation type	No. of respondents	% of respondents
County council	18	30
District council	15	24
Central government	5	8
Quango	7	5
Voluntary body	9	15
Private sector	4	10
Other	3	8
Total	61	100

The interviews concentrated on officers employed by the above organisations and the completed questionnaires reflect this. But, in addition to this survey, a small number of members was interviewed to obtain some feeling from elected members directly involved with these arrangements. Comments are interspersed throughout the report but it is suggested that more specific work needs to be carried out on the role of the locally elected member in inter-agency working to gain a more comprehensive picture.

In addition to providing a crucial input to the case study chapters which follow, the interviews can be used to assess overall attitudes to aspects of joint working. The number of respondents by case study is shown in **Table 2**. These numbers are not large but, given care was taken to identify respondents from a range of agencies, the interviews do provide evidence to underpin several general observations.

Table 2. Survey respondents by case study

Case study	No of respondents	% of respondents
Transport planning	14	23
Strategic planning	14	23
Community care	17	28
Environmental policy	16	26
Total	61	100

The average time spent on inter-agency working varies enormously — from 2% to 100% in our sample. **Table 3** shows a sizeable majority (84%) spend less than half their time on inter-agency collaboration. Many of our respondents carry substantial duties over and above their inter-agency commitments. Indeed, just over half of our sample spend less than 20% of their time on inter-agency working.

Table 3. Time spent on inter-agency working

Time spent	No of respondents	% of respondents
Less than 5%	4	7
5% to 19%	24	44
20% to 39%	9	16
40% to 49%	9	16
50% to 75%	6	11
Above 75%	3	6
Total	55	100

A critical factor is the level of resources that agencies can devote to joint working. As **Table 1** shows, more than half the respondents surveyed were working for county and district councils. One respondent noted: "Small districts do not have resources to cope with this kind of work." Another comment was: "This kind of work is more easily coped with at a county level, although district input will be important as this is where policies will be implemented."

As well as examining perceptions of the performance of specific collaborative arrangements, we asked respondents, based on their own experience, to rank the overall benefits and disadvantages of joint working. As can be seen from **Table 4**, the top three high-scoring benefits in our list were: enables participants to present a unified and stronger case to outside agencies and authorities; enables a better quality of outcome to be achieved; and enables pooling of

14

expertise to offer value for money and more effective working. However, all seven claimed advantages received strong support.

Table 4. Perceived benefits of joint working

Benefit	Recognised as a benefit % (number)		Not recognised as a benefit % (number)	
1. Enables participants to present a unified and stronger case to outside agencies and authorities	98.0	(48)	2.0	(1)
2. Enables a better quality of outcome to be achieved	95.9	(47)	4.1	(2)
3. Enables pooling of expertise to offer value for money and more effective working	95.9	(47)	4.1	(2)
4. Enables participants to resolve conflicts of interest	93.9	(46)	6.1	(3)
5. Overcomes artificial boundaries between geographical areas	91.8	(45)	8.2	(4)
6. Overcomes artificial boundaries between functional areas of work	89.8	(44)	10.2	(5)
7. Enables elected members to influence other agencies	68.8	(42)	14.2	(7)

Table 5 shows how respondents ranked the disadvantages of joint working. The chief complaints are that it slows down decision making and occupies too much officer time. One observation was that "work is tied to the slowest element" and the whole exercise can be slowed down where "officers have not got the executive authority required".

Table 5. Perceived disadvantages of joint working

Disadvantages	Recognised as a disadvantage		Not recognised as a disadvantage	
	%	(number)	%	(number)
1. Slows down decision making	83	(40)	17	(8)
2. Occupies too much officer time	73	(35)	27	(13)
3. Involves lack of public accountability	58	(28)	42	(20)
4. Is not able to resolve conflicts of interest	58	(28)	42	(20)
5. Takes power away from elected members	51	(24)	49	(23)
6. Offers poor value for money	50	(24)	50	(24)

Some of those interviewed commented that joint working can be more risky than having control through one organisation: "Relying on outside agencies can cause anxiety — they can let you down." Clearly, in some cases there was ambiguity about powers and ability to make decisions: "There is an uncertainty about roles and authority for agreeing action." A comparison of **Tables 4 and 5** suggests there is ambivalence on the part of some respondents regarding the strengths and weaknesses of joint working. For example, some respondents argued that joint working could both resolve conflicts of interests and also fail to solve conflicts of interest. They suggested that where important values were at stake it was possible that a joint arrangement which had coped adequately with minor tensions and difficulties could come unstuck.

We also asked respondents to rank six **potential** achievements of joint working and the results are shown in **Table 6**. The potential of giving an integrated approach to problem solving, perhaps predictably, comes out top. Interestingly, however, the potential for improving innovation and achieving added value also score highly. The potential for simplifying day-to-day management scores comparatively badly.

Table 6. Perceived potential of joint working

Potential	Strongly agree or agree	
	%	(number)
1. Gives an integrated approach to problem solving	94	(45)
2. Achieves added value	88	(42)
3. Improves innovation	85	(39)
4. Provides continuity for making decisions on cross-boundary issues	81	(38)
5. Improves responsiveness	72	(34)
6. Simplifies day-to-day management for tasks which need to be undertaken across boundaries	55	(26)

The research shows that, when asked to outline other benefits, a whole list of unexpected benefits occurred not often specifically related to the original objectives for the collaboration. Respondents often referred to an extension of understanding, the exchange of skills and expertise, and that "collaboration encourages people to think more broadly". This aspect of partnership working often acted as the stimulus for the professional officers to make a real commitment to making the joint working happen: "I benefited from the personal involvement — professionally it has extended my knowledge."

Table 6 covers aspects of effectiveness. Earlier it was suggested that accountability is also an important consideration. **Table 7** summarises responses to a question about the degree to which the public influences joint planning in practice. Some 38.5% felt the public had no influence at all, which lends support to the claim made earlier that networks may often be seen as aloof, if not downright secretive.

Table 7. The degree of public influence on joint working

Degree of influence	No of respondents	
	%	(number)
A great deal	23	(10)
A limited extent	38.5	(17)
None at all	38.5	(17)
Total	100	(44)

Conclusion

This section has provided a context for subsequent chapters. It has suggested that approaches to inter-agency collaboration are underpinned by different driving forces. In some situations, co-ordination may be imposed by the hierarchical exercise of power by a superior authority. In many situations, however, co-ordination is achieved through forms of trading and mutual adjustment. Agencies and actors can be seen to engage in a process of give and take which often requires changes in culture and approach, particularly where joint arrangements take in a broad range of agencies. Two over-arching criteria for assessing inter-agency collaboration — effectiveness and accountability — have been outlined. These criteria and the sub-categories within each are used to appraise the performance of the inter-agency arrangements discussed in subsequent chapters.

The research method has involved examining the practice of inter-agency collaboration in four contrasting policy arenas: community care; strategic planning; environmental policy; and transport planning. While the 61 respondents we have interviewed are almost all enthusiastic about the benefits of joint working, the discussion has identified some of the perceived drawbacks. The issues raised in this section are now examined in more depth in each of the four policy arenas.

3. Collaboration in community care

Introduction

Collaboration has long been seen as vital in the provision and development of community care. Some people need a range of health, social care and other services in order to live in the community; for others, the switch from one type of service (such as in-patient hospital care to home-based care) may mean that new services are required. In addition, an individual's social and health needs shift over time. If an individual's needs are to be recognised and addressed "in the round", it is essential for the various agencies to develop a co-ordinated response.

Also, in the community care field, the policies and actions of one agency can have major implications for other organisations. For example, the closure of long-stay hospitals can have profound implications for social services, housing and other services. Moreover, the emphasis on community care reflects a wish to support people in the community rather than in institutions. This suggests not only that the various statutory and voluntary agencies need to collaborate effectively, but also that they need to develop an improved capacity to listen to the concerns and priorities of service users and their carers.

This case study examines the experience of collaboration in community care by focusing on the planning and delivery of services for people with learning difficulties (or, as some prefer, people with a mental handicap). There has been considerable innovation in joint working in this policy arena for more than a decade and, by examining joint planning in two contrasting localities (South Glamorgan and Avon), the case study provides a number of insights on the strengths and weaknesses of alternative approaches.

Context

Joint planning and joint financing between health and local authorities was first introduced in England and Wales in 1976 but, in the early years at least, the results were not impressive. The original hope was that joint planning would secure the best balance of services and the best use of resources in meeting the needs of priority groups — including people with learning difficulties. A spur to joint working was provided by the concept of joint financing which enabled health authorities to contribute fixed amounts of expenditure to personal social services spending by local authorities. On the whole, the money was spent but it proved notoriously difficult to develop effective approaches to joint planning.

A particularly bold initiative designed to overcome the obstacles to effective joint planning and financing, which have worked against the development of comprehensive, community-based services for people with learning difficulties, was put together in Wales in the early 1980s. Launched in 1983, the *All Wales strategy for the development of services for mentally handicapped people* [18] set out to develop new patterns of more local services. In some ways the All Wales Strategy, now known as the Welsh Mental Handicap Strategy, pioneered approaches to joint working which were to be promoted nationally in the late 1980s. For example, the concept of "care management", which involves an across-the-board assessment of needs and tailoring of services to meet those needs, was a central plank of the 1989 white paper on community care, *Caring for people.* [19] However, the white paper also introduced proposals for the separation of purchasers and providers. Within health services the health authorities would do the commissioning and contracting and the self-governing trusts (consisting of hospitals and community health services) would do the providing. A similar separation was proposed for social services and social work departments, although no single model was laid down concerning the most appropriate organisational level at which this should occur. The NHS and Community Care Act 1990 legislated for these changes.

Under the new arrangements, health and local authorities have to prepare community care plans, known as social care plans in Wales, giving details of:

- The strategic objectives for community care
- The user groups for whom services are to be provided
- Assessment procedures
- How service priorities are to be determined
- Resource implications
- Quality issues
- The development of consumer choice
- Consultation arrangements.

While health and local authorities continue to be separately accountable for their performance, partnership and collaboration are seen as crucial. Clearly, it is important to assess how these new arrangements are working out in practice.

Impetus and objectives

The concept of "new patterns of comprehensive services" lies at the heart of the All Wales Strategy. The aim was to develop a full range of locally-based services and ensure those services were carefully co-ordinated and readily available to service users. From the outset there was a strong emphasis on consumer participation in the planning of statutory and voluntary services. The strategy has been governed by three principles which the Welsh Office reaffirmed in its 1992 publication, *The All Wales Mental Handicap Strategy*.[20] These are:

1. People with a mental handicap have a right to ordinary patterns of life within the community

2. People with a mental handicap have a right to be treated as individuals

3. People with a mental handicap have a right to additional help from the communities in which they live and from professional services in order to enable them to develop their maximum potential as individuals.

To put these principles into effect, planning and management arrangements have been developed at three main levels: the all-Wales level, the county level and the local level. At the all-Wales level, a crucial role has been played by the Welsh Office — particularly in relation to funding. The all-Wales arrangements have attempted to:

● Provide a mechanism by which the strategy is financed
● Assess the compatibility of locally prepared plans with the overall strategy
● Provide guidance on the preparation of and implementation of local plans designed to put the strategy into effect
● Encourage the pooling of ideas and information and to disseminate good practice
● Monitor and evaluate the development of services to ensure they adhere to the strategy.

There is no equivalent to the All Wales Strategy in England in the sense of a strongly articulated central government strategy backed by an earmarked budget. However, the inadequacies of arrangements for health and social care planning were identified in a number of highly critical reports about the implementation of community care in the late 1980s.[21] The seminal report on community care by Sir Roy Griffiths advocated the allocation of resources from the centre via a specific grant which, along the lines of the All Wales Strategy, would be conditional on the preparation of an adequate community care plan by social services departments.[22] While this proposal for a specific grant was rejected by central government, many of the Griffiths Report recommendations were accepted — including a statutory requirement to prepare, consult on and publish annual community care plans.

The Griffiths Report indicated that the fundamental purposes of community care plans were to serve as:

- Instruments for linking needs assessment with resource allocation
- Instruments for securing accountability.

In summary, we can note that the impetus behind moves to improve collaboration in the field of community care has come from central government. Voluntary bodies, enlightened professionals and civil servants can claim credit for lobbying central government into a more proactive approach going beyond the relatively ineffective exhortation of the 1970s. However, we can already see that approaches are rather different in England and Wales.

Organisational arrangements

There is no fixed pattern of joint working and collaboration at county level in either England or Wales. Indeed, the All Wales Strategy deliberately avoided imposing a blueprint. Rather the eight counties were encouraged to develop their own ideas. In the early years some counties had formally constituted joint care planning teams comprising representatives of health and local authorities, while others favoured a more loosely-structured approach to inter-agency co-operation. In practice all counties now have county joint planning teams (CJPTs). These teams, which comprise social services, health and education authorities, voluntary organisations, parents and representatives of service users, are required to produce three-year rolling programmes. These plans are prepared in line with Welsh Office guidance and include quantitative and qualitative measures of performance. It would be wrong, however, to imply that the Welsh counties have the same approach to collaborative working. There are, for example, considerable differences between counties in the extent and nature of voluntary sector participation — in much of rural Wales there was little or no voluntary sector at the beginning of the strategy. The involvement of housing and education departments is also variable.

Similarly there is no fixed pattern of joint working in England. Certainly all local authorities have had to produce community care plans — the first ones were produced in 1992 — and, within these plans, they have had to address the needs of people with learning difficulties. However, the particular way in which different agencies and groups are brought into the planning process is left to individual authorities to determine.

In England, no fewer than five central government departments are involved — Social Security, Health, Environment, Education and Science, and Employment. In terms of inter-agency collaboration at local level the main agencies which tend to be involved are:

- Social service departments
- The health authority
- The family health services authority
- Housing departments and housing associations
- Education
- Voluntary organisations
- Carers and service users.

In Avon, the inter-agency arrangements are as follows. In 1990, following the National Health Service and Community Care Act, the "purchasing" organisation (within the health service) was the Bristol and District Health Authority which has now been merged with the Avon Family Health Services Authority to form the Avon Health Commission. The "provider" organisation (within the health service) for people with learning difficulties is the Phoenix NHS Trust which gained self-governing status in April 1992. The Phoenix trust provides a diverse range of services — including hospital services, day services, residential placements and respite care. Similarly Avon CC social services department provides a range of residential, day care and support services. These are not the only key players: Bristol City Council housing department, a range of voluntary organisations and, of course, carers and service users are also heavily involved.

In 1994 an independent report by the National Development Team (NDT) examined proposals to close Avon's remaining long-stay hospitals for people with learning difficulties and concluded that the existing arrangements for inter-agency collaboration were less than satisfactory. Indeed, the report aroused considerable controversy and led to a radical rethink. In order to develop better integration of services for people with learning difficulties Avon Health Commission and the county social services department have introduced the new arrangements for inter-agency working (see Figure 1 overleaf). Key features are:

- The creation of a joint commissioning team to formulate and implement a joint strategy for the commissioning of services for people with learning difficulties in Avon. (This has its own office separate from any of the other agencies)

- An officer joint strategy group (bringing together health, social services and housing representatives) to advance strategic proposals and resource allocations through parent bodies

- A joint member steering group with members from Avon social services committee, Avon Health, two district councils, Avon People First (providing a voice for service users) and Bristol Community Health Council to advise on policy interpretation and to comment on strategic proposals and

23

Figure 1. Organisation for joint planning for people with learning difficulties in Avon (1995)

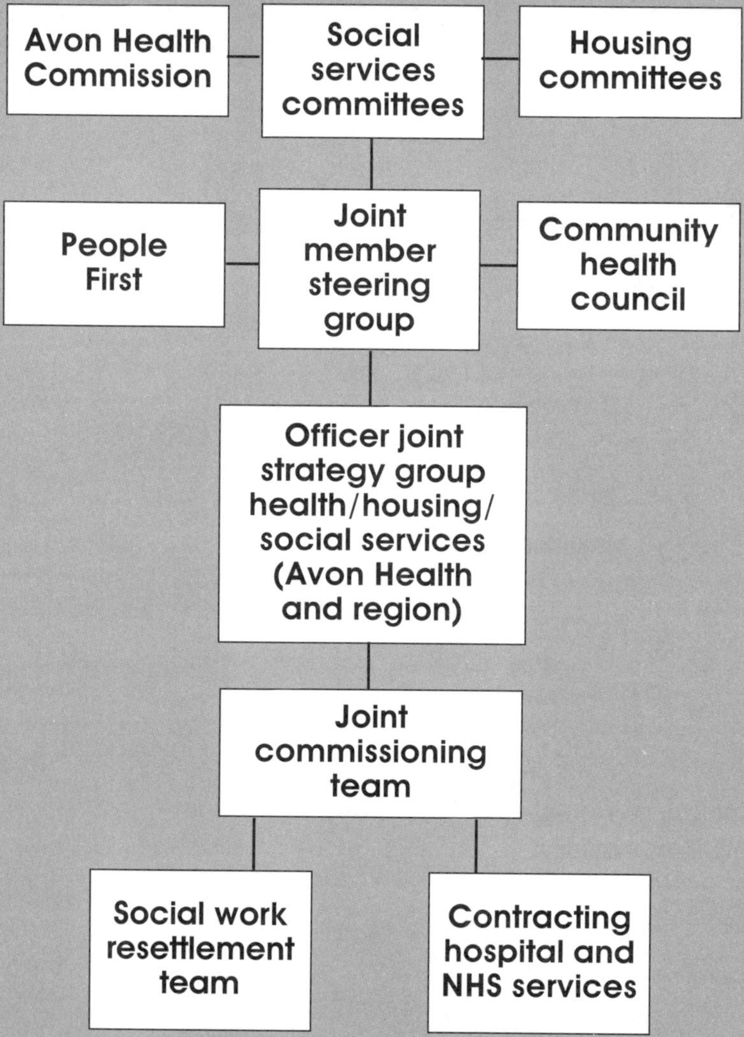

advise on policy interpretation and to comment on strategic proposals and resource allocation.

In South Glamorgan the organisational arrangements are rather different. When the All Wales Strategy was launched, a joint forward planning panel (JFPP) was set up to prepare the county plan. A joint management board (JMB) of officers was responsible for implementation. The JMB brought together officers who were able to commit their agencies and included representatives from: health, social services, education, housing (two districts), voluntary bodies and parents. A criticism of the JFPP was that it was unwieldy — some participants were there just to observe.

In more recent years the JMB has been replaced by a joint officers group (JOG) and the JFPP has been replaced by a joint planning and procurement board (JPPB). This reflects the requirements, set out in the National Health Service and Community Care Act 1990, to separate out commissioning and providing roles.

Evaluation

i) General
In general terms we can note that the All Wales Strategy encouraged Welsh local authorities to move ahead more quickly with imaginative community care policies in the 1980s than their English neighbours. A previous joint initiative in South Glamorgan, known as the Nimrod project, provided a prototype for the All Wales Strategy. Interviews with those participating in the innovations in South Glamorgan in the mid-1980s suggest that three factors contributed to the early success:

● A relatively coherent philosophy in the All Wales Strategy

● The availability of funds. In 1993-94 the All Wales Strategy budget was £48 million. This represents a fairly sizeable sum. "It was a ring-fenced sum and we would only be allowed to spend it if we reached agreement"

● Enthusiastic key players. Personalities can be critical and would seem to be an important factor in explaining the variation in performance across Wales. The overall research on the All Wales Strategy suggests some counties have pursued the policy with considerably more vigour than others.

In the Avon context, it is important to record that substantial changes were taking place while the research was being carried out. These stemmed from the National Development Team report of 1994 which pointed to a need to rethink and reshape approaches to inter-agency working. A new model, with a joint commissioning project team at its core, has now been introduced and this promises to bring about a more integrated approach.

ii) Effectiveness
In relation to objectives, the All Wales Strategy seems to have benefited from establishing clear principles at the outset. One respondent suggested: "We were all singing from the same hymn sheet." Others suggested that this was to overstate the level of agreement: "There was not so much shared vision as a clear framework for moving participants towards implementation." There was less agreement over ethos and objectives in Avon. One respondent suggested: "The regional health authority was not as clear as it needed to be about the role of the Phoenix NHS Trust when it set it up. As a result the trust seemed to go its own way and did not communicate that well with the other agencies."

This interpretation is challenged by the Phoenix trust which argues that Avon CC opposed the establishment of the trust and "boycotted the trust throughout the whole of its shadow period (November 1991-March 1992) and continued that boycott well after the April 1992 general election with varying degrees of intensity for another year". This was clearly not a happy period in inter-agency collaboration. The new arrangements aim to develop a shared understanding on objectives. One respondent suggested that: "The new joint commissioning team has the promise to develop a much clearer purchasing strategy, certainly as compared with the previous confusion."

In South Glamorgan the evidence suggests that the approach to joint planning within the framework of the All Wales Strategy represents good value for money. Mencap's remarks on the All Wales Strategy apply equally to the performance of South Glamorgan: "The new philosophy, new money and new services have made a striking impact on the quality of life for many people with a mental handicap and their families."[23] However, the charity takes the view that there is still much to do — hence the Mencap campaign slogan "a job half done". Some 78% of our respondents in the community care case study felt the arrangements for inter-agency collaboration represented good value for money.

So far as responsiveness is concerned we can note that the participation of different agencies has been uneven. The social services departments in both South Glamorgan and Avon have tended to take the lead. Health and housing services have also been key actors. Education has been spurred into playing a role in South Glamorgan but does not seem to be actively involved in Avon. In both counties steps have been taken to give a voice to voluntary organisations, parents and carers. In South Glamorgan the voluntary sector has played an active role in designing the planning structures. The new joint commissioning team in Avon represents a bold innovation in joint working. Its location in a separate office from the parent agencies is significant. The team has made a good start in developing a multi-levelled approach to strategic planning and has created new settings for working with stakeholders. This model promises to make new connections.

In relation to **stability and flexibility** there is a contrast between South Glamorgan and Avon. In the South Glamorgan context the arrangements appear to have been fairly robust over the years. In Avon the pre-1994 arrangements were found to be unsatisfactory and a new structure has been created — it is too early to judge how robust it will be. In both areas, as in the rest of Wales, Scotland and parts of England, new arrangements are having to be created in preparation for local government reorganisation. In Avon considerable progress has been made on creating new frameworks for partnership between the unitary authorities and the voluntary sector. Inter-agency area commissioning groups (ACGs) related to the areas of the new unitary authorities are now up and running. There is, however, widespread concern about the reorganisation. As one health official put it: "Local government reorganisation will slow us up considerably. There will be new members, new officers and, in many ways, a new start."

iii) Accountability
In relation to relating to the public it is helpful to distinguish the "interested" public from the public at large. The public at large may have little or no interest — certainly this was the experience of those involved in the consultation on the Avon Community Care Plan in 1994. However, the "interested" public — for example, parents and carers — can be expected to be much more willing to put time and effort into participation. This may be a useful distinction to draw in relation to public participation in joint planning arrangements in other policy arenas.

From the outset the All Wales Strategy emphasised the importance of drawing carers directly into the process of planning and managing services. In many counties, including South Glamorgan, there is a strong consumer voice in the joint planning arrangements. Similarly, the new arrangements in Avon stress the importance of working with stakeholders. A recent paper makes the following points about the approach adopted by the joint commissioning project team:

1) People using services have the clearest understanding about how well services are being delivered and what their own needs might be, now and in the future

2) There are a number of other individuals and organisations who have an interest in how services are purchased, and who should therefore be offered an opportunity to contribute their views

3) Purchasing of services will be enhanced by developing effective ways of working with users, carers, providers and other stakeholders

4) The views expressed by the various groups will be valued by the people making decisions about which services to commission and purchase.

There is a variety of ways of involving carers and users. There is some evidence to suggest that more progress has been made in the planning as opposed to the management of services. Even in the planning sphere, voluntary organisations point to weaknesses. As one respondent put it: "Participation can be tokenistic. It can also put a lot of pressure on a small group of parents and service users. It may professionalise these service users and it can get bogged down in details."

South Glamorgan has recently pioneered a variety of ways of involving parents and users in decision making. Parents and carers of people with learning difficulties have formed a federation and are being trained to join professionals in the monitoring and reviewing of services.[24] It has been decided, in principle, to reimburse them for loss of professional earnings while they carry out this work. South Glamorgan social services department provides training and support to the parents who join the monitoring and review teams. These teams, which bring together professionals, the voluntary sector and parents, visit and review six services a year. The experience suggests that these inter-agency teams have been effective in working across organisational boundaries, lifting the importance of user feedback and improving the operational responsiveness of services.

In relation to **political** accountability, the picture is rather different. In general the accountability to elected members in the All Wales Strategy has been flimsy. The professionals have been the main change drivers spurred on by voluntary bodies and carers. This may turn out to be a weakness. One respondent suggested: "Not enough was done to sell the message at member level. You have to get these ideas onto other people's agendas and we didn't do enough of that." For their part, the members interviewed seem to have been proud of the achievements and fairly content with a hands off approach. This may, of course, have been a benefit in that it allowed the officers to get on with the job.

In the Avon context it would seem that there is a higher level of member involvement. This may reflect the political cultures of the authorities involved, particularly so far as Avon CC is concerned. It also, perhaps, reflects the fact that the local authorities felt they needed to be proactive in sorting out what seemed to be an unsatisfactory situation.

In relation to **financial accountability** the inter-agency arrangements we studied appear to be sound. In both the South Glamorgan and the Avon contexts participating agencies have clear procedures for authorising expenditure.

Conclusions

A number of key points can be made about inter-agency working in this policy area:

1. Effective joint planning and joint working is essential if there is to be any hope of meeting the needs of people with learning difficulties

2. Because of the complexity of the task, the joint arrangements are, inevitably, complex and this puts considerable demands on those responsible for joint working

3. There is a long history of joint working in this policy area going back over 20 years, so there is a good deal of experience to draw on

4. There is wide variation in practice and some particularly interesting differences in the approaches adopted in England and Wales — for example, the Welsh Office has been a key change driver in Wales

5. There is considerable innovation not only in collaboration among statutory agencies but also in collaboration between statutory agencies and the voluntary sector

6. There is some innovation in user and carer involvement and, while carer representatives argue that there is much more to do in this direction and many professionals agree, there is some useful experience which may be relevant to other policy areas

7. There is a high level of concern about the anticipated disruptive effect that local government reorganisation will have on established patterns of inter-agency collaboration

8. There are major challenges in bringing together professionals from different organisational cultures and this places a premium on mutual learning and staff development

9. While it may be difficult to get all participants to agree on a joint vision it is possible clearly to set out areas of agreement about future provision and agree the necessary steps to achieve this provision.

4. Strategic land-use planning

Introduction

The research focused on two geographical areas and looked at two comparable organisations that are currently operating on a regional/sub-regional basis. Both use the term "conference" in their title to denote long-standing arrangements and both are local authority based and have been established primarily around county councils to fill a perceived vacuum at a strategic level. They are also comparable in that, although their core area of activity is land-use planning, the organisations have spread their wings in taking on a wider remit. The two organisations operate on a political level and a technical level and are essentially working to a formalised structure within the framework of voluntary joint working. Budgets for the organisations are small, composed of member agency contributions, and essentially both conferences are mechanisms for co-ordination and collaboration rather than direct providers.

The research looks at two specific pieces of work (recently carried out and completed by the organisations) as vehicles for understanding the nature of the operation, and therefore allowing retrospective consideration of the arrangements in the context of this study of joint working. For south Wales, the research looked at the *Renewable Energy Study Policy Guidelines*.[25] The study was jointly commissioned between the conference and the Energy Technology Support Unit (part of the Department of Transport and Industry), prompted by *Planning Policy Guidance Note 22*.[26] The work was undertaken by a combination of technical officers from local authorities in south Wales and landscape consultants. The purpose of the study was to produce policy guidelines for individual local authorities to apply throughout south Wales.

For the south west of England, the research focused on the regional guidance exercise for the region. In order to inform structure planning, the Department of the Environment (DoE) requested the conference to undertake the required work on producing the guidelines. The process, in practice, has not been plain sailing, as following the original draft guidance produced by the conference, there were disagreements between the DoE and the conference as to its contents. These differences have now been resolved, largely due to the combined efforts of several senior offices in the member authorities and the DoE regional office. The guidance has been agreed and is now operational.[27]

Context

Strategic planning lends itself particularly well to joint working, especially where there is a vacuum in Britain at the sub-regional/regional level of any formal statutory organisations for planning. There has been a long history of joint working arrangements being established across local authority boundaries for strategic land-use co-ordination and also addressing special strategic issues.

Recent deliberations on local government reorganisation, along with the re-emergence of the regional debate in the UK, have put strategic planning in the spotlight. The abolition of the metropolitan councils in 1986, and the impending disappearance of the regional councils in Scotland, have focused attention on models of working generally based on voluntary arrangements. A number of local authority groups currently operating in the UK are attempting to fill the strategic gap in the administrative framework, and the two organisations at the centre of this study are very typical of the general approach in terms of scope and structures. In a recent discussion paper, the Association of Metropolitan Authorities (AMA) states:

> "Local government has responded positively to the increasing importance of regionalism. The contribution of the regional associations of local authorities has been particularly important."[28]

Although committed to a non-statutory regional structure, central government has made some moves in recent years to respond to regional needs and has found that existing local government groupings are useful vehicles. Both organisations being considered in this research have been seen by central government as suitable for specific activities and this pattern has also emerged in terms of relationships with the European Union, particularly in bidding for funds, where some form of regional plan and framework is required. In the same report quoted above, the AMA refers to "creeping regionalism" and says that the level and scope of activity by local government, and at a conurbation and regional level, reflects many factors including:

> "The regional agenda of the government, its agencies and the European institutions, particularly the Commission and the Committee of the Regions."[29]

It is also worth pointing out that local government regional/sub-regional associations are a vehicle for networking, campaigning and raising awareness and "identity". Again, with the lack of statutory structures, voluntary local authority inter-agency groups are often the only means available for consultation and feedback on specific regional or sub-regional proposals. For example, the newly-created rail franchise process has used both conferences for the purposes of enabling regional consultation on proposed rail operations.

Impetus and objectives

The impetus for setting up both organisations under consideration has come primarily from the reaction to a spatial strategic gap in the formal administrative structures in the geographical areas of south Wales and south west England. The arrangements could be considered as standard local government responses in terms of structures, machinery and processes. The setting up of the organisations came from within local government itself at the county council level, and primarily derived from concern over planning issues. In fact, the South Wales Conference, in its original title, included the term regional planning which was later changed to regional policy, indicating a broadening of subject area for the conference.

The objectives for both organisations clearly rest in achieving closer co-operation between local authorities on strategic issues such as structure planning. In addition, the aspect of liaison with central government is important — these joint agencies operate at the interface between central and local government. The South Wales Conference has taken a more proactive stance in that its objectives include the aim of devising joint policies. This appears to have been achieved in limited subject areas, and more obviously on topics where there is likely to be a general consensus across the sub-region.

Organisational arrangements

In terms of their original objectives, both organisations have broadened somewhat. South Wales in particular is tackling European and transportation issues, and the conference has taken on a strong campaigning and lobbying role on behalf of the area, the campaign for the second Severn crossing being a good example. South Wales is a more homogeneous region, both geographically and politically, than is its counterpart in the south west. The large and disparate area of the south west of England, that extends from Gloucester-Cornwall-Dorset-Wiltshire, does make some issues of joint policy difficult. For the South Wales Conference there is a clear identification with the traditional sub-region of industrial south Wales.

Both organisations draw their membership from local government, unlike other sub-regional groupings, such as Clwyd Economic Forum in north Wales, which include voluntary organisations and private-sector agencies in their membership. Both organisations use a formal secretariat with one key officer who acts as the overall co-ordinator. However, the bulk of the technical work is carried out by professional staff in the partnership organisations. Occasionally this is supplemented by the use of consultants, as in the case of the Renewable Energy Study where specialist consultants were employed. The structure of both conferences includes political and technical representation, with elected councillors from the participating councils being the responsible decision-making group with advice coming from the technical officers. For both conferences there are sub-grouping arrangements among the officers specialising in particular policy areas, such as transportation.

Evaluation

i) General
Overall, the general impression is that both organisations have worked well in their remit of filling the strategic vacuum. This point was stressed time and again by respondents — for example: "There is a vacuum at the regional level and we are doing our best to respond." Many people feel that local government is actually taking on the responsibility that should be carried out by central government in the absence of proper regional government, for example: "We are giving a lead in local government."

However, there were recognised limitations to the arrangements, partly due to the budget, as in south Wales, or because of the difficulty of keeping "everyone on board". This was recognised to be a real problem in the south west, particularly due to the geography. Unlike south Wales, where meetings are rotated around the area, Somerset remains the focal point of the south west: "Everything happens in Taunton — it takes two hours there and two hours back; there is a limit to how much officer time we can commit on this basis." Thus the very thing which binds them together as a spatial grouping — geography — can be an obstacle to participation. The principle of the organisations being voluntary was also a critical one. It was clear that issues that were bound to raise widespread disagreement between the participants were largely avoided by not being included on the agenda. Even for those issues that are put on the agenda, the conferences per se do not have any executive power, For example: as one officer interviewed pointed out: "On aspects which are controversial, authorities make up their own mind and can choose to ignore voluntary corporate working."

Strong operational similarities exist between the two conferences. The objectives, arrangements and processes are directly comparable and it could be said that they represent joint working that is a typical, local government approach to a perceived geographical need and on a subject area firmly in the remit of local government. Care had been taken to set up formal structures which allowed a defined process to take place and there was little evidence that any of these mechanisms had been ignored or by-passed. There was a general feeling that both organisations operated in a spirit of goodwill between the local authorities, and a high degree of co-operation and consideration was shown:

"The model is a good one but does rely on a high level of personal motivation. This can impose a heavy workload on those officers involved in joint working." It was pointed out that joint working between officials in central and local government was more difficult, generally because those in central government seemed to have less room to manoeuvre. This was felt particularly strongly in the south Wales example on renewable energy where joint resolution of approach was essential: "Local government had to make the compromises."

ii) Effectiveness

Setting and keeping clear **objectives** is seen as critical for achieving effective joint working: "The main objectives have to be agreed for joint working." For both organisations, the research showed that all respondents were able to clearly articulate the objectives for the arrangement and these were understood by all participants. This, in practice, allowed a common purpose to be established which set directions for the joint working. This may be because for each of the arrangements considered, there was a finite programme, timescale and budget.

All but one of the respondents felt that joint working represented good **value for money** and 100% said it gave added value. The renewable energy study particularly was seen as a pooling of resources with the comment that "on their own, no one authority could have afforded to carry out this work". However, it should be pointed out that both organisations operate on "officer contributions that go uncosted" but the sharing of loads or responsibilities allowed equal participation and benefit. For south Wales, the standing conference overall was seen as being very beneficial in carrying out joint research or policy development, which gave member authority contributors "added value". This was often referred to as "a better outcome" or the added value of bringing people together, producing new ideas. For smaller authorities it is often the pooling of expertise which gives their added value.

In terms of **responsiveness**, there was a more mixed view from respondents. Some felt the structure was not particularly responsive and did not innovate. Setting a common goal was an advantage but it was difficult to introduce change at a later date. While 100% of respondents felt joint working resolves conflict of interest between participants at the technical level and could be responsive in this way, this was not thought to be true at the political level. In addition, there was frequent comment that responsiveness was diminished with central government involvement, although in the south Wales case there was considerable flexibility shown by the quango involved and it was clear that officers had more freedom to operate.

The setting of clear objectives and structures gave both arrangements a comprehensiveness in approach which was reinforced by the discipline of reporting back within a local government structure. However, when looking at the organisations overall in terms of their ability to be effective in a comprehensive way, it was very interesting to note that again, with the exception of one respondent, everyone thought there was an inability of the organisations to resolve conflicting political objectives. What emerged from interviews with key players in the organisations is that the scope and agenda of the two conferences is drawn to avoid those issues that may cause deep disagreement among members. In this way there is an imposed limit to the comprehensiveness of the organisation, and as the member agencies work on a voluntary basis, nothing is binding. One of the members interviewed stressed that the function of the joint working is "advisory". This aspect of being advisory emerges as a potential weakness in terms of implementation of joint policy.

Looking at **stability and flexibility,** both organisations had proved to be long-standing and were very stable. The Welsh Standing Conference had lasted for nearly 30 years, although there is now a question mark over its future due to local government reorganisation. The South West Conference had its roots in the structure planning exercises in the 1970s but became a formal body in the 1980s, incorporating Devon and Cornwall in 1989. Therefore, in terms of stability, the conferences have been continuous and, despite financial cutbacks in local government, all the members had stayed on board in terms of contributions. The individual arrangements looked at in detail had again appeared easy to maintain; all the technical contributors had been required to be there by their employers and there was little evidence of anyone straying from the objectives or agreed programme. This probably says something about the nature of local government in Britain, in that it does provide an effective framework for getting certain work done. Many respondents commented that the biggest threat to the organisation came not from budgets or a lack of commitment, but from local government reorganisation which would change local authority structures in both areas.

As previously noted, both organisations devised a very similar management structure which revolved around a small secretariat acting at the centre and operated on the basis of technical working groups led by named officers. There was agreement from participants that the designated leader approach worked. Several respondents picked on particular management problems. For example: "There is no sanction on those who do not contribute to the work — often imposing a heavy workload on others." In addition, a large number of respondents felt the arrangement was heavily dependent on the work of one or two individuals.

In relation to the Renewable Energy Study and the Regional Planning Guidance, the outcome was seen as the production and approval of the relevant policy document. The quality of that outcome is difficult to ascertain. For the renewal energy policy, the participants thought the document was a good one but there were fears about implementing the policies on the ground. Already one non-participating district council has said it will not be bound by the recommendations. Similarly, there were reservations at the district council level on the south west guidance. This indicates one of the real dilemmas of these voluntary groupings — they have no real implementation power and, as mentioned above, attempts to implement at the regional/sub-regional scale on the basis of goodwill can be difficult.

iii) Accountability

In terms of **relating to the public** this emerged as a critical issue in the research. From the interviews carried out it became clear that a comprehensive framework for accountability had not been thought through in a structured way by either organisation. A specific question, asking the extent to which the public could influence the exercise, was answered by all respondents as either "none at all" or "limited". No-one thought the public had been given any real opportunity to influence the exercise. In fact, for many respondents it became clear that this was the first occasion the question had been raised. In the south Wales study, this was even more interesting due to the fact that the subject area of renewable energy (in terms of windfarms) was highly controversial and had, in fact, raised huge public attention in parts of south Wales. There was, of course, the standard "reporting back" mechanism through council minutes but this, in practice, can be a fairly tenuous route.

If we differentiate between the general public and interested public (as noted earlier in the report), the South West Conference had made attempts to make the decision-making process more accessible by raising public awareness and making direct contact with the interested public of their area. The press were used to publicise the regional guidance exercise and seminars were held to limited audiences who were thought likely to have an interest. In addition, the county councils then consulted with district councils and other agencies on the basis of a county forum. It was agreed that to raise responses from the general public on strategic issues was very difficult to do and in an area like the south west was practically impossible. However, there does seem to be a real acknowledgement in the south west of the need to get information out to a wider community. In addition, county forums provide the opportunity for a regular dialogue between the county and district councils.

In both organisations there was a direct mechanism of **political accountability** through the elected members. The chairs of both organisations were given a strong role in terms of day-to-day activity — and certainly for south Wales it appears that technical direction is stronger than political direction — but there was obviously a close working relationship between the chair and the technical officers. There is a slightly different pattern for the south west where certainly the Liberal Democrats organise as a group for the conferences and clearly give it a high political priority.

36

In fact, for both organisations, political involvement seemed to be very much at a directional level. Where agencies outside local government became involved, it was generally believed that "elected members have more limited control". Locally elected members have little influence over other outside organisations because of the complexity of the arrangements. Politicians appear to operate a clearer mechanism of accountability in the south west with an emphasis on reporting back. For the South Wales Conference, political lines of accountability can be more diffuse and, with the meetings at quarterly intervals, raise questions of matching the timing of decision-making meetings with those of participating authorities.

For both organisations there was a clear and direct structure for **financial accountability**. However, with these two examples it must be remembered that overall budgets are small. Budgets are often specific to identifiable pieces of work, as in the Renewable Energy Study, and "can act as a controlling factor".

Conclusions

It was clear from the study that both of these organisations were fulfilling what was generally considered by all those approached to be a very useful role in the topic area of strategic planning where co-operation is seen as vital. The evidence is that, within the confines of a voluntary framework and limited resources, organisations like the South West and South Wales Conferences can achieve defined objectives. However, there are inevitably constraints on these organisations, particularly in terms of operating in subject areas where agreement among participants would be difficult. It is clear from the research that areas which are anticipated to give a high degree of internal conflict are avoided from the outset. It must also be remembered that the voluntary nature of the co-operation means there is no means of enforcing decisions on member organisations and implementation of joint decisions cannot be guaranteed.

In addition there are some specific key points about the organisational structure and processes that are worth noting:

1. Setting clear objectives and mechanisms for achieving these objectives at the outset are fundamental for securing understanding, co-ordinating work programmes and ensuring outcomes. This was particularly true for strategic planning exercises that have a specific goal

2. There is a need to establish a focus for the organisations (which tend by their nature to be loosely knit) as a mechanism for driving on the organisations. Establishing a central point of administration and responsibility helps to give that focus. However, it is important that the organisation is given sufficient recognition within all member contributors otherwise there will

not necessarily be a sense of partnership or indeed of ownership of joint decisions

3. At the technical level the professionals involved were generally enthusiastic about their own personal benefit in working with others on a wider canvas. In particular, planners felt it had been a "good learning exercise". However, internal work pressures on staff were increasingly putting them in difficulties in also working on "outside" joint projects and it is, therefore, important that such joint working is given due recognition

4. In terms of public accountability, processes need to be made clearer and more thought given to opportunities, mechanisms for participation and feedback

5. The role of the local politician is often obscure in practice in joint arrangements. Political frameworks and mechanisms, and also responsibilities, need to be made clearer, otherwise many locally elected representatives can be sidelined or end up with no effective role. This can then contribute to the lack of a sense of ownership in the decision-making process outlined above

6. Neither organisation had much of a public profile although attempts had been made to establish themselves with the press. This is not surprising given the nature of the organisations, the subject area and limited resources, and it may be that the absence of a profile is not critical. However, there may be an increasing need to establish a clear and widespread identity as a means of locating themselves within the geographic and political decision-making structures which may help to encourage local interest.

The work of these organisations needs to be viewed in the overall context of a greater emphasis on partnership and joint arrangements that are seen to give benefits, particularly in terms of administration. Local government reorganisation has focused attention on the need for joint working on strategic planning. Although the government is showing increasing signs that it recognises the need for sub-regional co-operation, the current local government reorganisation which, in some areas eliminates county councils, is seen by some as reducing the strength of strategic planning. In these circumstances the role of voluntary local groupings may prove to be of greater significance and, perhaps importantly, local government reorganisation could also provide the opportunity for thinking through the mechanisms and operation of the joint arrangement, particularly to allow wider participation. Despite some of the fears about reorganisation, it seems likely that there will continue to be voluntary joint working on strategic planning partly due to the obvious common sense advantages of co-operation. As expressed by one south Wales councillor: "I think the conference is essential for south Wales — we need to work together."

5. Corporate environmental policy and initiatives

Introduction

This case study is concerned with the inter-agency working which occurs in the area of corporate environmental policy, sometimes known as local government "greening". Evidence has been collected at two levels. First, regional networking by local authority environmental co-ordinators has been examined. In Wales the Welsh Environmental Co-ordinators Forum now exists to facilitate this. In addition, mainly because regional networking tends to be for mutual support and information exchange rather than to achieve particular actions, attention has been focused on inter-agency working at local level where the establishment of an Energy Advice Centre in Cardiff and an environmental centre in Bristol have been investigated. Both cities have been active in developing corporate environmental policy. The two levels of inter-agency working are linked through the environmental co-ordinators who participate in both.

Context

Corporate environmental work is largely discretionary, although there are close links between non-statutory action and the well-established statutory environmental responsibilities of local government. Traditional environmental health and planning functions are increasingly pursued in the context of a new environmental agenda which embraces global as well as local issues. Recently, environmental strategy work has undergone a refocusing in pursuit of sustainable development.[30]

Tackling the new environmental agenda, which is broad and not easily compartmentalised, requires the development of corporate and strategic policy approaches. Practice is uneven. However, many authorities now have a strategy for action. Types of action linked to an environmental strategy include, for example, corporate energy policies, recycling initiatives, pollution monitoring, nature conservation policies and the greening of the council's own activities — for example, by encouraging employees to use public transport.

Organisational changes to support these policy developments principally include the creation of cross-cutting administrative and political structures within local authorities and the establishment of new posts. Many local authorities now have an environmental co-ordinator to take forward the new green agenda. These individuals play a key role in inter-agency collaboration in the field of corporate environmental policy.

Of particular significance is the development of new ways of working in partnership with agencies outside local authorities and with local communities. Partnerships are increasingly common for policy development (for example, in strategy formulation), service delivery (for example, in the area of recycling) and in carrying out environmental projects. During the course of this research project work on Local Agenda 21 has begun to give new impetus to inter-agency collaboration.

In addition to local arrangements for inter-agency collaboration, local authorities are increasingly engaging in networking for sustainability. Networking is both informal and formal, within the UK and internationally, attracting encouragement and financial support from agencies keen to see the exchange of information and innovative practice.

Impetus and objectives

Inter-agency working at the regional level
The Welsh Environmental Co-ordinators Forum — "a network of specialist managers responsible for the development and implementation of corporate environmental policies" in the local authorities of Wales — was set up in October 1991. The reported objectives — although these were not formally set out — were for the officers responsible for environmental co-ordination to share experience and practice, and to encourage the participation of Welsh authorities which were not then active in this policy field, especially by persuading elected members to give greater priority to environmental issues.

Although there have been no changes in the nature of this arrangement, further objectives have emerged. In particular, the forum has provided a vehicle for raising the profile of environmental work with the Welsh Office. Representatives of the environment division of the Welsh Office attend meetings and the group is now often consulted on environment division initiatives. The co-ordinators have also sought to ensure the continued development of corporate environmental policy in the new unitary authorities. Through written material and a conference held in Swansea in 1994 they have succeeded in influencing official guidance on the arrangements for corporate environmental management following reorganisation.

A more subtle objective for the Welsh forum relates to some participants' view of environmental co-ordination as an area for professional development, and perhaps even as a new profession.

All authorities in Avon (six districts and the county council) have an environmental co-ordinator. Like their counterparts in Wales, these co-ordinators network among themselves but they have not set up a particular arrangement for this and, in practice, they rarely meet as a group.

Local initiatives

Cardiff's environmental strategy has been in place since 1989. The council has a cross-departmental environmental strategy officers' working group and an environmental strategy members' working group which reports to the policy and resources committee. An environmental co-ordinator, located in the chief executive's department and appointed in 1991, provides a link between these two working groups. An environmental forum was formally established in 1992. The environmental co-ordinator is involved in international networking, especially through the Eurocities network, and in regional networking through the Welsh Environmental Co-ordinators group.

The Cardiff Energy Advice Centre is one of a network of local energy advice centres (LEACs) supported by the Energy Saving Trust. The trust was set up in 1992 "to identify, promote and manage energy efficiency schemes in the UK" as part of the national programme to reduce carbon dioxide emissions. Under a three year pilot scheme which began in October 1993, each local centre provides free independent advice to householders and small businesses on energy saving and the reduction of fuel costs. The Cardiff EAC, which employs a centre manager and two full-time workers, opened to the public in April 1994.

Examination of the joint working to set up the Cardiff EAC has revealed five key initial players: Cardiff City Council (through the environmental co-ordinator and the energy officer), British Gas, the electricity company SWALEC, the Cardiff Bay Development Corporation (CBDC) and the Welsh Development Agency (WDA). The two city council officers have taken the lead throughout.

The impetus for the centre came from two directions. On the city council's side, the initiative began with the Ecosave campaign in 1992. This scheme encourages energy saving by households by monitoring energy consumption in the home. The council was seeking a more strategic approach to energy management generally and was participating in an existing Energy Efficiency Office network. The Ecosave campaign brought the council into closer contact with the privatised energy utilities. With British Gas and SWALEC, the city began to discuss the possible establishment of an energy centre. At about the same time the WDA and CBDC were working on their own proposal for a telephone-based regional energy efficiency service based in Cardiff Bay. When the LEACs scheme was launched the city council officers — with some difficulty, since at the time rivalry among the players was quite marked — engineered a joining of forces.

As part of the national scheme, the Cardiff EAC itself has clear objectives. In addition, each of the funding partners interviewed expressed clear motives for their involvement in the project. For the council, the centre is a delivery mechanism for both the environmental strategy and the anti-poverty strategy. For the privatised utilities, the centre is part of marketing strategy and there are straightforward commercial aims. Additionally, support for the centre enables the utilities to fulfil obligations to their respective regulators. For CBDC, participation represents a good public relations opportunity for relatively little work.

In Bristol, the management structures for environmental policy within the city council have recently been subject to review and it is now claimed the city has a "model structure" for formulating and delivering corporate environmental policy. Leadership is provided by the health and environmental services (H&ES) directorate, and the city's environmental co-ordinator is located within the directorate's green initiatives team. There is a cross-directorate officers working group at senior level, attended by the chair and vice-chair of the H&ES committee, and this committee has overall responsibility for environmental matters. However, green initiatives are the responsibility of the green initiatives joint sub-committee, a sub-committee of policy and resources.

Bristol's *Green Charter*, launched in 1991, spells out the council's commitment to community involvement and partnership working for sustainability. The main vehicle for community involvement is the environmental liaison group (ELG), set up in 1991. From the council side, the members of the group are councillors rather than officers. It is a consultative body dealing principally with policy matters. It is not responsible for implementation, which happens through the mainstream functions of the council. Nor is it a vehicle for actions which require partnership approaches. The main forum for practical partnership working under the *Green Charter* is intended to be the Bristol Environment and Energy Trust (BEET).

BEET was set up in 1993. Its mission is "to integrate private, public and voluntary sector organisations in an action plan to minimise adverse impact on the environment, improve the quality of life and create the framework for sustainable development". The trust is funded by a three-year DoE Environment Action Fund grant matched with equivalent cash and in-kind support from its trustees. The trustees and members of the BEET steering group are drawn from the business community, local government and voluntary organisations. The work of the trust is organised around a number of action groups, including one ostensibly set up to foster the development of an environment centre, CREATE.

The inter-agency working to set up the CREATE centre has been examined in this case study. When the study began it was expected that work would focus either on the ELG or BEET. However, during the fieldwork it became apparent that, although much inter-agency working has occurred over several years with the aim of setting up an environment centre in Bristol, this has taken place via a number of ad hoc groups of individuals and organisations rather than through these more formal structures which have been set up relatively recently. In practice, as in the case of the Cardiff EAC, particular officers of the city council have been the key players.

CREATE has its origins in two strands of environmental work developed in Bristol since the early 1980s: waste recycling and energy efficiency. The initiative which has led to the development of CREATE was originally for a recycling centre. It came in the mid-1980s from the Recycling Consortium, itself a grouping of the Sofa Project, Resourcesaver and the Children's Scrapstore. This group made several unsuccessful approaches to the city council seeking a site for a purpose-built centre. Eventually a list of council-owned buildings with potential for conversion was made available and the B Bond warehouse was selected.

A study by local architects based on extensive consultation with potential users articulated the vision of the CREATE centre as a multi-purpose environmental visitor centre. Large-scale funding was needed and most potential sources require the demonstration of a partnership approach. Some structure was also required to manage the project. The idea of setting up a formal, cross-sectoral partnership was conceived. In the event, however, the council obtained supplementary credit approval from the DoE for £0.5m to set up a recycling centre. Since the money had to be spent fast, the council engaged a private developer to undertake the rapid conversion of B Bond. Ironically, perhaps, the building proved unsuitable for recycling, partly for planning reasons. This is not as disadvantageous to the recycling groups originally involved as it might appear. The lengthy inter-agency work preceding the conversion of B Bond, resulted in each recycling organisation obtaining improved premises from the council, so by the time CREATE came into being, they were relatively well-suited.

A number of organisations, including BEET, now have premises in the CREATE centre, and the city council has located its green initiatives team there. The centre is seen as a key part of the delivery of the council's *Green Charter*. An aim in setting up the centre is to foster inter-agency working among the users. In total, Bristol City Council has now committed £1.2m to the project. Further development is expected to occur incrementally as funding becomes available.

To summarise, the impetus for the inter-agency working surrounding the CREATE centre is multi-faceted and there has never been a commonly agreed set of objectives. Development of the centre is described as "spasmodic, ad hoc, disorganised, opportunistic" and participants are uncertain as to who is shaping

43

its future. However, the need for a strategy and business plan has been recognised and these are in preparation. The Chamber of Commerce is meanwhile preparing a marketing strategy for BEET which is expected to recommend that BEET and the CREATE centre are jointly promoted.

Organisational arrangements

Since the first meeting in March 1992, the Welsh Environmental Co-ordinators Forum has met twice a year, with the Powys co-ordinator acting as convener and secretariat. Although there is some formality in this arrangement — for example, the forum has a logo and agendas are agreed — the meetings themselves are informal in style.

Attendance, which is at the discretion of individual officers, is good with about half the Welsh authorities represented at meetings. Decisions about the work of the forum are made at the meetings but a small core group may take action between times.

In Avon, collaboration among environmental co-ordinators is on an ad hoc basis in order to undertake particular projects or it occurs simply because the co-ordinators know each other. A group meeting convened by the county in May 1994 had no particular agenda and no minutes, attracted criticism for being "too free form" and did not lead to any action. However, the co-ordinators are sometimes invited to meetings arranged by other organisations. For example, all but one attended a meeting of the Avon Environmental Education Liaison Group in March 1995.

The establishment of a semi-formal regional arrangement similar to the one in Wales may so far have been inhibited by the generally strained political relationships between the county and the districts, and between certain districts, especially in the context of the local government review. To set up a forum requires an organisational lead but if Avon CC does this, it is perceived to be dominating the agenda. Additionally, the recent entry onto the scene of BEET seems to have complicated the picture, since there is an expectation that partnerships at both regional and local level will be fostered by this agency.

In the case of the Cardiff EAC, the focus of research has been the EAC steering group, set up in June 1993, initially to prepare the application to the Energy Saving Trust. Membership of the steering group includes the five local funding organisations and representatives of several other organisations — such as Arena Network Wales and the Cardiff Chamber of Commerce — which have become involved more recently. A representative of Cardiff's Environmental Forum also participates. The current role of the steering group is to "come up with ideas for practical projects related to energy efficiency". A separate company with a board of directors exists to manage the project. In particular, financial management is the responsibility of the board. The board includes representatives of the funding organisations and it is chaired by a city councillor.

The steering group meets on an ad hoc basis, the secretariat being provided by the manager of the EAC. The group is officers only and its recommendations must be approved by the board of directors. Additional informal arrangements exist for both decision making and day-to-day working, essentially to allow the centre manager a degree of independence.

In Bristol, despite "an awful lot of collaboration and trust and compromise all the way through" there has never been one structure for the inter-agency working which has eventually produced the CREATE centre. It was intended that BEET — specifically established as an inter-agency partnership — should project manage CREATE. In practice however, the building is council-owned, the centre was developed by the council and the council is currently responsible for managing it. BEET is seeking involvement in other partnership projects across Avon.

Evaluation

i) General
In the environmental policy field a great variety of arrangements exists for inter-agency working. Regional networks of environmental co-ordinators have mainly been established to provide mutual support to participants, spread good practice in this policy field, gain credibility for innovative practice and lobby central government.

The Welsh Environmental Co-ordinators Forum provides much evidence of fruitful collaboration. However, it is significant that the participants — who typically spend a large proportion of their working time on inter-agency working generally — do not think of the forum in this way: "The forum is atypical of my inter-agency working. For me, inter-agency working is not the forum." What is seen to count as inter-agency working seems to have two key attributes: the involvement of agencies from more than one sector and seeking funding for particular projects. It is partly for this reason that the research effort moved to consider local joint working for particular initiatives.

ii) Effectiveness
Considering firstly **objectives**, arrangements with a clear set of shared objectives are likely to be more effective than those where objectives are not unanimously agreed or where participants pursue separate agendas in the context of the joint working.

Lack of a clear strategy can hamper joint working. This currently appears to be the case in Bristol for both the CREATE centre and the development of a role for BEET. However, strategy development is in turn seen to be hampered by an uncertain financial climate. Perceived empire building on the part of certain participants is believed by some voluntary groups to have influenced Bristol City Council in its decision to use a private developer for the CREATE building conversion and to manage the project in-house.

The Welsh forum works well partly "because people are not coming along with hidden agendas". It is worth noting here the Welsh Office comment that at points in the local government review process, when the counties and districts ceased co-operative working in mainstream environmental services, the environmental co-ordinators continued to meet as usual. This was put down to their shared commitment to the environmental movement and to group solidarity.

Commitment to the inter-agency working is linked to the perceived relevance of the joint objectives for the participants' own organisations. In the case of the Cardiff EAC the shared commitment of British Gas and SWALEC is interesting because the different fuel suppliers have traditionally been competitors: "Now we have a common bond because of the drive to energy efficiency." These points relate closely to feelings of ownership of the joint working. The Welsh forum is very much owned by the co-ordinators themselves, in contrast to the central/local environmental forum established in England which is perceived as central-government driven.

It is to be expected that participants making a large financial investment in a joint project will feel themselves to be owners of it. This is certainly true in the case of Bristol City Council in relation to the CREATE centre. However, the Cardiff EAC presents an interesting contrast. There, the Cardiff City Council representatives are perceived by other stakeholders to be the key players despite the fact that their financial contribution has been modest when compared, for example, with that of the CBDC. CBDC's interest in the project has reportedly been somewhat difficult to sustain.

Turning to **value for money**, a distinction needs to be made between the costs of running the various networking arrangements and the costs of outcomes. In general the arrangements examined here represent good value for money in that the running costs of meetings are minimal in relation to the benefit participants gain. Locally, partnership structures enable local authorities to access funding sources which they could not apply for if they were acting alone. Funding for the Cardiff EAC represents a case in point.

For the CREATE centre, views differ on the question of value for money. Over the years, both voluntary organisations and the city council have spent large sums on consultancy. At least one cross-sectoral bid for European funding was unsuccessful. The voluntary groups now located in the centre benefit from minimal or zero rents, so for them the whole project represents excellent value. On the other hand, they question the use of public money for this project: "Pouring half a million pounds into the council's own bonded warehouse on the edge of nowhere, which you can't get to and no-one knows it's there — that's not good use of public money."

On **responsiveness**, these arrangements can score highly. Responsiveness may be interpreted as contributing towards added value. Where participants in the inter-agency working provide services, networking has reportedly improved responsiveness to service users because the organisations have acquired expertise or knowledge through their contacts. In Bristol, participation in BEET, which brings together public, voluntary and private sectors, is particularly valued for this.

The participating organisations also gain directly from the networking itself: "Initially I got flack from my own organisation [for spending time on inter-agency working] but via all this networking we now have planned management and funding so we're OK to the year 2000 and its **because of** inter-agency working. We have picked up expertise and the confidence to deal with the private sector . . . "

The harnessing of specialist skills and knowledge was particularly highlighted by participants in the Cardiff EAC. Having specialist advice on hand via the steering group is seen as important for the effective functioning of the centre.

The joint arrangements themselves, however, may be perceived as insufficiently responsive to market conditions. This concern lies behind the following comment from one private-sector participant: "The only thing which worries me about joint working is its ability to respond to change. In my company . . . we have to respond to change all the time. In the past all decision-making was by committee — it worked well. But today we are frustrated by committees. These days they can get in the way of taking decisions forward."

At both regional and local levels an informal operating style is adopted, regardless of the degree of structural formality in the arrangement. The Welsh forum "works well because it is so informal — it's a friendship of people sharing similar problems". Informal working alongside a formal structure is seen as an aid to decision making. In the case of the Cardiff EAC: "It helps discussion at board meetings because you have the background to what's going on."

As in other policy fields, **stability** is related to the number and type of participants and to the degree to which objectives are shared and jointly owned, not least because these are in turn factors which determine how simple or difficult it is to manage the arrangement in question. Generally, agreement with the objectives is a more significant factor than the number or type of participants.

Potentially, inter-agency arrangements in the field of corporate environmental policy are straightforward to manage because of the shared vision and commitment of participants regarding environmental action. Decision making is generally consensual. Strong leadership is perceived as less vital than "just someone who pulls things together".

The formality of the arrangement and availability of resources also have relevance for stability. Once a trust or a company has been established, for example, and funding gained for a period of years, as in the case of the Cardiff EAC, a degree of stability is to be expected.

Effectiveness may also be related to the competence of individual participants and to the confidence which the stakeholders have in them. Members of the steering group for the Cardiff EAC, for example, expressed confidence in the centre manager to take day-to-day decisions which are then discussed and rubber-stamped by the steering group and management board. In the case of the CREATE centre, the council's apparent concerns about placing management of the centre in the hands of BEET may be a factor inhibiting the development of inter-agency working itself.

Finally in this section, it is useful to comment on the effectiveness of the outcomes of the inter-agency working, since this is particularly stressed by participants. Whatever voluntary groups may say about their apparent exclusion from the final stages of development of the CREATE centre, for example, and the fact that the facilities there are not precisely right for their needs (BEET, for example, is temporarily located in what is supposed to be the creche) they are happy to see the centre up and running. As one participant from outside the council commented: "In terms of activities, a lot is going on and the building is well-used. It's actually working despite the lack of overall co-ordination."

iii) Accountability
It is in the area of accountability that the arrangements for inter-agency working in the environmental field are most open to question. This is partly because few arrangements exist for monitoring and review except in cases where public expenditure is involved. In the case of the CREATE centre there are at least two issues for monitoring: "One is the development of the building as any other office development — there is financial monitoring and review. But these other issues — partnership — how the building is working to foster collaboration — there is no monitoring. They're just assuming that it will [achieve partnership] but there is not yet a critical mass of organisations."

There is room for improvement in **public accountability** but this is not seen as an immediate issue since the groups themselves are not constituted as public bodies. Paradoxically perhaps, while the public are virtually excluded from participation in the arrangements and strong efforts are rarely made to keep them informed, an important aim of these groups is enhanced community participation, especially for Agenda 21. The centres in Cardiff and Bristol are intended as public buildings, indeed as venues for public participation in environmental action.

The public do have an opportunity to learn of these activities through normal council channels. For example, the establishment of an environment centre was part of the Bristol local plan which was subject to formal consultation. If a project is successful in putting in place something that will be for public benefit, does it matter that the public are not **directly** involved in setting it up?

In Cardiff there was some consultation through tenants' organisations and the environment forum in the early stages of the EAC project. The principal means of public involvement is now the monitoring system set up for users of the centre. Regular returns are collated and published by the Energy Saving Trust, and "public reaction is central to the way the centres are being managed".

Political accountability is also potentially an issue. Where participants in these arrangements are council officers or elected members, normal reporting lines apply, though reporting arrangements specifically for the inter-agency working are virtually unknown. This seems to be true regardless of the degree of formality of the networking. In the case of the Welsh forum, which is an officer-only arrangement, the absence of councillors and, indeed, very senior officers, from participants' employing authorities is perceived as a benefit, allowing unconstrained discussion. The Welsh co-ordinators have themselves discussed the question of accountability in relation to their increasing consultation role. They claim a professional right to comment — in the manner of a professional organisation such as the Royal Town Planning Institute — rather than political legitimacy.

A particular problem may arise where private trusts have been set up to run environmental projects or services. Despite the participation of elected members on steering groups and boards, these structures tend to be perceived as undemocratic and unrepresentative. During this research, questions of political accountability have especially been raised in relation to BEET, in which the city council is but one of a number of stakeholders.

In the voluntary and private-sector organisations consulted, there again seems to have been little reporting back to trustees, management boards, directors or shareholders specifically on the inter-agency working except where legal issues — such as leases — have been involved.

Financial accountability is not an issue in the regional arrangements described here since the sums involved are minimal. It is, however, important when public funds are used in environmental action, as in the case of the environmental centres in Cardiff and Bristol. In Bristol, this is the key factor in the council's concern to maintain control of the project. Clearly, appropriate structures for financial management need to be set up to safeguard the interests of funding bodies. The arrangements for the Cardiff EAC demonstrate that such structures can work well.

Questions of accountability and effectiveness are evidently linked. If appropriate structures are in place and if the individuals concerned have appropriate skills, direct involvement of elected representatives, shareholders or the public is not necessary for accountability: "At the end of the day someone needs to make a decision and carry the can, otherwise it's unworkable. If you've got the right people appointed — the right expertise — it should take care of itself really."

Conclusions

In this policy field, inter-agency collaboration is seen as vital. In the most general terms this is because environmental issues straddle both administrative and sectoral/professional boundaries. However, there also exists a shared vision of sustainability and strong personal commitment to environmental action on the part of the key players. This is evidenced by the participants' preparedness to "keep plugging away", in some cases over a number of years, to achieve a desired goal, and to spend many hours outside paid work-time in networking with others. Much progress is being made outside formal structures by means of informal contacts among the participants.

The important role of key actors in progressing inter-agency working is also striking and questions may be asked about the continuing momentum of work if certain players leave the scene.

From a political point of view, the green policy area differs from others in that it attracts wide public and political support. On the other hand, this area attracts a wide range of actors so that arrangements for inter-agency working may involve some "strange bedfellows". Difficulties arise where certain partners are weaker than others in terms of resources or influence, and where the working involves several such groups they may compete among themselves for influence in the context of the joint working.

In considering the involvement of different sectors in the inter-agency working for sustainability, it appears the private-sector commitment is less than that of either the public or voluntary sectors. It may simply be that local businesses get involved in partnerships elsewhere — such as in local business and environment clubs. Bringing together the two policy fields of environment and economic development is an important contextual aim.

In this policy area, the role of the local authority is by no means clear cut. Agencies outside the local authority may take the initiative when the authority is perceived to be slow to act. On the other hand, local authority contacts see themselves as enablers/facilitators in this policy field when in fact they are likely to remain firmly in control of both inter-agency structures and practical initiatives.

It is conspicuous that the key local authority actors in the arrangements studied here are officers rather than members, despite the generally positive view of joint working for corporate environmental policy expressed by the councillors interviewed in both Bristol and Cardiff. There has been little direct involvement of elected members in the establishment of local environmental centres. However, political support and guidance at critical points in the process of inter-agency working are seen as vital to progress.

There are also points to be made about organisational culture. For some groups, the aim is to foster inter-agency working itself — to achieve synergy — and to achieve cultural change within the participating organisations, and not necessarily to undertake particular work. It is also considered important that participating organisations share certain cultural values, such as a commitment to equal opportunities and to democratic processes.

Lastly, observations in relation to inter-agency working for corporate environmental policy may have relevance for current thinking about organisational change in local government. For example, external partnership arrangements tend to be tied in to cross-departmental organisational structures in local authorities at both officer and member levels, as vertical hierarchies are replaced by horizontal arrangements in this policy field. Many environmental organisations have flat management structures and very co-operative management styles. These fit well with current thinking on good practice in environmental management. Some senior local government officers — as well as environmental co-ordinators — are converts to the "sustainability vision". They see themselves as no longer part of the traditional professionally-based hierarchy and have adopted a style of working which relies heavily on informal networking with outside groups, both to gain personal support and to achieve practical outcomes.

6. Inter-agency working in transport

Introduction

The policy area of transport provides a good case study since it comprises a number of activities which are undertaken across geographical and functional boundaries. Furthermore the responsibility for transport lies with a range of government agencies, local authorities and private-sector companies, often working in collaboration across sectoral boundaries. The transport sector has historically worked across geographical boundaries to reflect journey-to-work and other established travel patterns in their areas.

Collaboration has occurred particularly at the strategic transport planning level, ranging from research and policy development to service-level planning and provision. For the provision of public transport, joint working has been a key element of local activity and in some cases these have been formalised into a defined organisation, as in the passenger transport authorities (PTAs) set up under the Transport Act 1968. In more recent years, joint working between agencies has been encouraged by the Department of Transport as a basis for transport funding.

The case studies chosen for the research represent current aspects of joint working between a variety of agencies, including different tiers of local government and also central government. Essentially the research concentrates on examples of collaboration in the preparation of transport studies. The Cardiff Region Public Transport Study, led by South Glamorgan CC, and the Black Country Integrated Transport Study both take in a range of agencies, including transport operators. In addition to looking at these two studies, the research has also looked at a particular package bid that was put together for the West Midlands. This is a useful example of how joint working can operate in practice as a means of enabling service delivery.

Context

There is a range of joint working models operating in the UK which are intended to achieve strategic integration in transport planning and management. As mentioned above, for the metropolitan areas there are PTAs with formal statutory boards. There are also less formal groupings, where co-operation is secured through voluntary arrangements, usually to achieve specific tasks. In addition, there are also many examples of jointly-funded specialist units or agency arrangements that can be managed, where needed, by joint committees. In Wales many local authorities are currently working alongside or with quangos such as the Wales Tourist Board and the Welsh Development Agency to secure transport objectives.

A variety of recent incentives for collaboration in the transport area should be noted. First, the opportunity to win grants and support, especially for infrastructure, from the European Union, requires proof of a partnership approach. Deregulation and privatisation can be said to have both a fragmentary and, contradictorily, a collaborative effect on service provision as partnerships have emerged over time between county councils and private bus operators. The same pattern may well emerge post-railway privatisation, although, at present, considerable uncertainty surrounds the future of railways.

The recent publication of the government's *Policy Planning Guidance Notes on Development Plans and Regional Planning Guidance* [31] and on transport[32] not only indicate greater policy integration at a central level, they also require transport and planning authorities to work more closely together. The emphasis of meeting targets on sustainability arising from the 1991 Rio conference and initiatives being pursued through Local Agenda 21 all emphasise the need for joint working on transport issues.

Impetus and objectives

There is a whole range of reasons driving joint working in transport, with local government often co-ordinating and pushing these initiatives. The objectives of these ventures tend to revolve around two core points: first, achieving better quality of service delivery; and second, in terms of either using or acquiring financial resources. The examples studied clearly respond to both objectives.

Importantly, the manner in which government funds are currently allocated through the transport supplementary grant encourages a package approach. This is based on the advice of the Royal Commission on Environmental Pollution which recommended a balancing package of investment to increase the capacity, convenience and reliability of public transport which is environmentally less damaging.[33] This kind of approach, originally initiated in the West Midlands, has been required by the Department of Transport to be underpinned by an integrated transport study. For this reason, the approach taken in the West Midlands is useful as it has been in operation for several years. In metropolitan areas, in particular, authorities are encouraged to work together across former metropolitan county areas, and joint bids between districts and PTAs are effectively mandatory in metropolitan areas.[34] In the Cardiff study, the impetus is more on patterns and forms of public transport delivery in the future but the study is likely to lead to funding bids.

Organisational arrangements

The Cardiff Region Public Transport Study was initiated in 1992. The study was financed by a group of agencies, including two county councils, two district councils, Cardiff Bay UDC, the Welsh Office, Regional Railways and the Confederation of Passenger Transport. The study carried out by consultants has been overseen by a group of officers led by South Glamorgan CC with an evolving structure of sub-committees or working groups to progress particular aspects of the work. There is no limited timescale for the arrangement as there is a series of on-going studies which it is intended will ultimately lead to bids for major resources to implement a public transport strategy for the area.

In the context of the arrangement, there is no formal structure for joint member involvement and the process has been for the study to be reported back to members in the local authorities as major conclusions have been reached. In this respect the study has been treated as a very technical piece of work, although it has required considerable inputs of resources and clearly does have political implications — both in terms of funding the study and subsequent design developments — which will require very large sums of money.

In contrast, there is a more formalised structure operating in the West Midlands and there is an overall joint committee of members that approves the submission of the West Midlands Transport Package Bid. This has representatives of seven adjoining councils. In 1992 the Department of Transport agreed to consider a joint bid from the seven West Midlands councils and Centro as a result of their previous collaborative work. Centro, the West Midlands Passenger Transport Executive, which has a degree of independence, acts as a mediator bringing together the local authorities and the government office for the region. It is worth noting that the executive is the officer arm of the organisation as contrasted to the PTA which is composed of members. The West Midlands Joint Committee had been set up "to support the various authorities aims for the development and well being of their area". It is composed of member representatives of the contributing agencies and is completely separate from the PTA. The research has focussed on the preparation of the bid to the Department of Transport as a means of considering how this joint arrangement works in practice.

The other part of the research has looked at the Black Country Integrated Transport Study which, in a similar way to the Cardiff study, has drawn a group of agencies together for a specific purpose. The four metropolitan borough councils, Walsall, Wolverhampton, Sandwell and Dudley, along with the Black Country Development Corporation, the Department of Transport and Centro, came together for the specific task of producing a study with no apparent intentions for the arrangement to continue beyond this. Like the Cardiff study, it has no member steering group or joint committee and it was overseen by a group of technical officers drawn from each agency with reporting back mechanisms through each individual participating agency.

These studies have been chosen for the research as they represent typical models of joint working arrangements that have been put in place for transport. The three are similar in character but are set in different geographical and political settings.

Evaluation

i) General
It is evident from the interviews that the joint arrangements have largely met the needs of participating agencies. Respondents are clearly impressed by the achievements of joint working (92% felt it worked well in practice) and in general did not identify specific difficulties or shortcomings in the arrangements. A high percentage thought joint working had enabled a better quality of outcome; and a common view is that joint working in transport is typically established to achieve substantive objectives that would be difficult, if not impossible, to achieve with a single authority. For example, in relation to the Cardiff study, no single authority could impose the radical solutions to urban traffic growth and congestion which can be developed through the collaboration of several agencies.

However, some reservations were expressed over the detailed procedures associated with joint working. For example, there were reservations about the way informal working took place within the studies and there was a feeling that procedures are less well defined than they could be. Another example which emerged in the research was that joint working in reality can confer executive powers on officers in the absence of clear mechanisms for reporting back to politicians. This often gives a freedom for officers in which to act. It was suggested by one respondent that such authority can be usefully exploited by officers to improve the efficiency and effectiveness of joint working.

ii) Effectiveness
There was general agreement that those involved in the joint working arrangements understood and agreed with the **objectives** of the exercise. However, there was a feeling that some people still pursued their own objectives, too, and the operational mechanisms were not always able to resolve conflicts of interest between the different agencies. In particular, in the West Midlands there was some tension between the Black Country authorities and Birmingham. It seems clear that the Black Country study had been prepared as a reaction to the previous Birmingham study. It is interesting to note that the same Black Country authorities then joined with Birmingham to work on the overall West Midlands Package Study. In this context they had to resolve their differences for the best strategic outcome.

In terms of financial benefits, three quarters of those interviewed think overall joint arrangements represent good **value for money**. In practice, for these studies, technical participation tends to take place at senior/chief officer level and it was generally thought this enabled speedy decisions to be taken between the agencies and, therefore, was financially effective. In addition, for the West Midlands example there was evidence of the effective harnessing of European and central government money.

In relation to **responsiveness,** joint working is considered to offer opportunities for innovation and this partly results from joint arrangements bringing together a number of technical specialists who are not typically available to a single authority. There was virtually unanimous agreement among respondents that joint working allows the pooling of expertise and more effective working as a consequence. In the words of one interviewee: "Joint working delivered a better quality decision in the end as a result of collaboration." In fact the majority of respondents felt that enhanced quality of outcome was the most beneficial advantage of joint working.

In terms of how the joint arrangements operate, particularly in terms of the **stability and flexibility** of the arrangement, it emerged that the effect of one or two people leading the way was important. It is clear from the interviews that there was an acceptance by most that the lead agency concept was effective. Three quarters of those questioned thought having a designated leader is critical to the effective working of the arrangement. For example: "The success of the package approach is attributed to the personal commitment of key individuals."

But a significant number of those interviewed felt the work was very heavily dependent on one or two individuals. In terms of the stability of the arrangements, clearly, where needed, the arrangements are continuing. This in itself indicates that these are reasonably strong arrangements which can meet their objectives. For the West Midlands Package Study, in particular, bids for funding will be an ongoing feature and, while current funding policies appertain, will require some form of joint agreement. In terms of the ability to sustain these arrangements in the long term, there was concern that joint working did take up considerable officer time and this was seen as a considerable disadvantage by those involved. This raises questions of methods of operation and how workloads are distributed internally in agencies. It is interesting to note that the West Midlands package process has been ongoing every year. Authorities have continued to submit joint packages despite a majority of authorities having changed political control, even while packages were being put together. From this it would appear that the contributors all felt the joint approach was certainly beneficial.

iii) Accountability

In terms of **relating to the public** it seems the public are often consulted. For example, in the case of the Cardiff study there was a major consultation exercise on the study's initial conclusions. But it is often after decisions have been made that the public are consulted or are asked to comment on alternative options, rather than the desirability of a more general policy direction. Half of our respondents felt the public had no influence on the arrangements at all. It is not clear, however, that this arises out of joint working per se — it is common to the type of project or activity which such arrangements in the transport sector are set up to address.

In relation to **political accountability,** those interviewed felt joint working at officer level did not compromise accountability. More than half of the respondents did not agree with the view that joint working involves a lack of accountability. This is consistent with the stated belief that key decisions, particularly those on funding or policy, are passed through the committee structure of each participating authority. For example, in the Cardiff case study when the consultants report is submitted it goes to various working groups as the authority sees fit. These groups have elected councillors on them. Eight respondents out of 14 feel joint working does not take power away from elected members. Of those who do believe this to be true, only one respondent ranked this as a significant disadvantage. However, it should be noted that these are views of officers — we were unable to check the views of members within the time-frame of the project.

With the development corporations, their boards have responsibility for decision making on those matters relating to the joint arrangement. In general, the procedural benefits that officers derive from the lightness of reporting back mechanisms are not felt to be at odds with the maintenance of effective accountability. But further work on the views of councillors is needed.

In relation to **financial accountability**, procedures appear sound. In the case of the West Midlands package approach, Solihull holds the "pot of money" and distributes it among participants as agreed by the joint working group. The participants must then report back to Solihull on spending performance.

Conclusions

The benefits of joint collaboration in the transport field were shown to be very strong in these case studies. These are examples of a common approach now being used on integrated transport studies in the UK. The need to agree collaborative action in order to gain funds and to integrate transport delivery are clearly powerful incentives to work together — in the West Midlands it was a mechanism for an effective local government voice in the way central government funds are allocated. In these circumstances, agreements were reached on the basis of collective decision making, which at times obviously puts pressures on the individual agencies as decisions on priorities had to be made.

Some points emerged that were particular to the transport area:

1. There is, to an extent, a difference in the professional culture between public transport planners and highway planners who often have a contrasting view on transport priorities. This can be a problem in joint working and these issues need to be addressed at an early stage to reduce potential conflict.

2. Joint working is particularly appropriate for project based exercises which have a defined purpose and a specified timescale.

3. The lack of substantial political involvement was not thought to be a hindrance in developing and achieving joint projects. On the whole, public involvement was not seen as critical in the research stage but could be incorporated as a consultation process at the end of a project-based approach.

4. The transport work was seen as highly technical, with benefits at the officer level of working together in a specialist team and without strong political constraints.

However, in terms of some of the procedures adopted for developing these studies, there may be a need to think through the public and political framework for decision making if these joint working procedures are to become long-standing arrangements.

7. Key themes in collaboration

Introduction

Joint working in the public sector now involves a very wide range of agencies. This reflects the multiplicity of decision making and the jigsaw of agencies which are operating in Britain today. The reality is that inter-agency working has grown in importance and much greater attention needs to be given to methods of operating across administrative and responsibility boundaries.

The detailed research work undertaken, as well as providing illuminating information and conclusions on individual topic areas as outlined in the previous four chapters, has also produced some clear themes and issues which underlie current practice. These themes are interesting in that they are not only pertinent to many of the current debates on structures and processes for policy formulation and service delivery, but also relate to current debates taking place on the role of regionalism and the challenges facing local democracy. This chapter considers the following cross-cutting themes which emerge from the case studies:

- The role of central government
- The role of regional government
- The role of local government
- The role of non-governmental organisations
- The role of the private sector
- The role of the public
- The architecture of joint working
- The influence of resources
- Managing cultural realignment
- Identification and ownership
- Innovation.

The role of central government

The research suggests the role of central government can be critical in inter-agency working and can help or hinder the outcomes. The pattern of central-local relations is complicated in practice as central government now has both a Westminster and varying regional forms. In the case of England, it seems the regional directors are gaining increased discretion to form effective partnerships with local agencies, as exemplified in the South West Planning Guidance. In the Welsh context, this discretion was less clear as the civil servants still work to a secretary of state as a member of the Cabinet. In this way, the current relationships between central, regional and local levels of government are varied.

On the positive side, the research showed central government can be a change-driver where local agencies have largely failed to get together. For example, the role of the Welsh Office in the All Wales Strategy for people with learning difficulties, coupled with the incentive of finance for service delivery, acted as a powerful stimulus for joint working. One voluntary sector respondent argued: "In 1983 the Welsh Office was well ahead of its time. It needed to be prescriptive. Demanding three-year plans with the carrot of cash was a power-ful incentive for people to work together." Clearly, then, central government has a legitimate and potentially valuable role in stimulating joint working at local level.

The downside of this argument is that, as in the case of the All Wales Strategy, too much reliance may have been placed on the Welsh Office. The signs are that the Welsh Office wants to step back from a leadership role on the grounds that the local agencies should now be up to the job. In part this could be a pragmatic response to the fact that there will be 22 unitary authorities in exis-tence in April 1996 (as against the eight counties at present). But there is a widespread view that the problems run deeper and that progress in the next few years could falter: "The disadvantage of the 1983 style of joint planning is that it is seen as Welsh Office owned. The resources were good but local polit-ical ownership has been neglected. There are real fears that politicians on the new unitary councils will not be interested."

It has also been suggested that central government uses inter-agency networks of collaboration very much for its own purpose and imposes a top-down view rather than one derived from a local base upwards. In this way, joint working may become a convenience for central government rather than a means of increasing the scope of local government. In addition, it was felt that there was always less flexibility with central government: civil servants seem to be more constrained and this can be a real obstacle to progress. It was felt that, where there was conflict between the central/local government dimensions, it was always at the local level that "accommodations" had to be made. In terms of the role of local members, the reality of this kind of decision making means locally-elected members are having less control and influence on the outcomes.

Also, central government can disrupt existing arrangements of joint working. For example, the implementation of local government reorganisation will have this effect on the ground. It may result in the imposition of joint boards, as was the case in the metropolitan areas and in London after 1986. It will certainly disrupt established patterns of joint working. And central policies appear to be pulling in different directions. For example, unitary authorities are smaller than counties while health, probation and police are being asked to serve larger areas. This makes co-operation across organisational boundaries more difficult.

Our research suggests that central government needs to consider more carefully the impact of central decisions on local networks and collaboration. It is clear that the centre can be force for good in acting as a catalyst to bring about joint working. For example, by requiring proof of joint working before making financial awards, as with transport supplementary grant, the centre can promote effective collaboration. But, in an increasingly centralised state, Whitehall needs to take great care to leave sufficient political space for local innovation and initiative.

The role of regional government

Throughout the research, the use of the term "strategic" in the geographic sense has been repeated and, certainly in the cases of strategic planning and transport planning, the need for co-operation at the regional or sub-regional levels has been a critical driving force. It could be argued that the present joint working arrangements, although doing a reasonable job, are second best to a formal structure at the regional level. In terms of public accountability, it is clear from the research that direct and obvious lines of accountability often do not exist and in some ways the voluntary arrangements are partial and difficult in practice. Joint boards can make the picture clearer but tend to be topic-based and do not necessarily relate to other subject areas.

As mentioned earlier, the government offices for the regions are now developing a more defined regional layer. While the government officers for the regions were given the remit of "working in partnership with local people", they are also to "play a crucial role in delivering the government's policies in the regions". It remains to be seen where the emphasis will be in terms of a top-down or bottom-up approach to regionalism. Current debates about regional councils and assemblies have raised the possibility of setting up structures which make responsibility and powers more explicit and may lead to more effectiveness due to their clearer political control. However, in much of the current thinking there are still questions as to how outside agencies, now a key factor in policy formulation, could be brought into the regional framework.

By comparing and contrasting inter-agency working in Wales with south west England, the research has pointed to the differences between the Welsh Office and the Government Office for the South West. It would be wrong to imply that Welsh experience can be easily exported — it is not easy to see how every English region could have a secretary of state in the Cabinet. However, the research has shown that in some areas of policy — for example, the All Wales

Strategy for People with Learning Disabilities — the Welsh Office was able to work creatively with local authorities, and other agencies in Wales helped to foster local networks and government. For the regional office structure, it is too early to make conclusions but clearly it does provide a platform for closer working with local government and other agencies.

The role of local government

The research has shown that local government has acted across a whole range of subject areas as the catalyst for inter-agency working. This was particularly clear in, for example, the transport package approach, where administrative boundaries are very subsidiary to travel movements on the ground. It is often at the local level that the inadequacies of fragmented service delivery and structures of implementation are identified, and, therefore, it is not surprising that joint working is often promoted as a method of problem solving.

Local authorities can also offer important knowledge and resources in relation to joint working, both in terms of ways of working, and skills and talents. One of the interesting facets of change in local government practice (often due to external forces) has been the need and ability to work within a wider network of agencies. Community care, for example, illustrates the important interlinking role that local government must play. The skills and knowledge that are developed by local authority officers, alongside in-depth specialist knowledge, tends to equip local government to play an effective role in a wider network of joint working. All our case studies suggest local authorities have been key actors in developing collaborative models.

This networking can be carried one stage further where decentralised structures are in place by developing joint working models over a range of spatial and service arrangements. The involvement of local government can also be an important catalyst for change and innovation. This, again, was shown clearly in some of the case studies. For example, local authorities can be found pushing health authorities forward in the area of community care, and campaigning on issues of public concern — for example, on traffic congestion in cities. Local government has also played a critical role in developing and delivering an environmental agenda. This is clearly brought out in the examination of the Cardiff Energy Advice Centre and the CREATE centre in Bristol.

However, there are still difficulties in local government which need highlighting as being negative or potentially detracting from the successful outcome of inter-agency working. Entrenched departmental and professional attitudes can work against effective inter-agency collaboration — for example, the divide that may exist between planning and transport, and indeed between highways and public transport planners.

Local authorities may see inter-agency working as an "add on" and sometimes as a peripheral issue to the local authority itself. This may be particularly true where inter-agency working is part of a contracted out model. Methods of reporting back are critical here, otherwise processes of accountability are often overlooked or the arrangement is not only perceived but also becomes peripheral to the work of the authority. This is particularly true for voluntary arrangements where the activity is not seen as part of the mainstream work of the local authority.

In terms of elected members, this can sometimes mean authorities do not nominate their most effective members to these outside organisations. This may indicate just how seriously or otherwise the council is in terms of its commitment to the arrangements. Overall, it became clear from the research that the role of elected members in inter-agency working is rarely thought through properly, and this is a critical issue both in terms of the role and membership of councillors.

From the research carried out, member participation in the wider activities of local government, including the local government associations, very much depends on the availability of time. For most members with limited time available, their efforts tend to be concentrated on the priorities of their own authority and the electorate; there is little scope for a regular and deep involvement on a wider canvas. This does raise important concerns about the structure of local government for the future and needs further thought and clarification. Recent work by the Commission for Local Democracy touches on these points but does not really illuminate issues of joint working.

The role of non-governmental organisations

In reality, NGOs now play an active role in influencing and informing decisions by government at all levels. In addition, as in the case of community care or environmental activities, they may have the role of direct providers. Partnerships have evolved in many areas of service delivery, such as recycling or in providing environmental education and awareness, as in the case of the CREATE centre in Bristol. In many cases, NGOs are serious stakeholders in joint arrangements. They provide an important link to service consumers and can be a catalyst for innovation. Their weakness may be that the more informal groups can suffer from instability and their input into joint arrangements can wax and wane, often depending on funding and on personalities. However, the more formal and structured NGOs, especially where they are operating on a contractual basis, are often key partners in joint working and are reasonably stable in terms of their ability to be involved over a long period of time.

Special mention should be made of the valuable contribution made to joint working by voluntary organisations and representatives of service users. This is particularly striking in the field of community care. Our research in this area suggests that the voluntary sector can make a vital contribution to policy formulation as well as service provision. Also, new organisations, such as federations of parents and carers, bring new ideas as well as direct experience of problems "on the ground". Effective inter-agency working needs to draw in the voice of service users — good practice in the sphere of community care has lessons for other policy arenas. With care and attention, it is clearly possible to bring excluded voices into the decision-making process.

The role of the private sector

Compared with north American and other west European experiences, the private sector in the UK has had a relatively limited role in local governance. But increasingly, it is starting to become involved in partnership arrangements at the local level. As well as contractual service roles through CCT, there is now a growing area of experience with defined joint working on policy development and research — particularly in the sphere of local economic development — between the private and public sectors. However, the private-sector actors often have a specific agenda and need to see clear outcomes to encourage participation.

This is obviously the case in the transport example where direct involvement is seen to be critical for survival. In other areas of work, where the outcomes are not specific, it may be difficult to sustain private involvement. It may be that less demanding mechanisms should be put in place — for example, one-off seminars or specific research projects — which are more attractive to private bodies, as is the case in the south west strategic planning context. Significant private-sector involvement in inter-agency working may require traditional models to be rethought. If the issue of defined results is a key factor for the private sector, familiar approaches to joint working may be found wanting.

The role of the public

In Chapter 2 it was noted that 38.5% of our respondents felt the public had no influence at all on joint planning in practice. There is certainly a sense that the often complex arrangements set up to handle joint planning and management are perceived as impenetratable, even arcane, by outsiders. For example, the case study on corporate environmental policy and action suggests that public involvement has been low, despite the fact that the projects studied are intended to provide venues for public participation in environmental action.

The experience of community care may provide some useful pointers. The All Wales Strategy, for example, placed a strong emphasis on user and carer involvement. The research uncovered bold examples of innovation in this area with high levels of public involvement. The research has suggested that it may be helpful to distinguish "the interested public" from the public at large. It is clearly the interested public which has provided energy and impetus for innovations in community care. It may be that those concerned with inter-agency working should focus their attention on the interested public if they wish to strengthen the citizen's voice in decision making.

The architecture of joint working

A considerable amount of research has been carried out on formal structures of joint working, particularly statutory joint boards and committees.[34] However, in practice, Britain has seen a wide range of working arrangements develop which, although having a formal basis, nevertheless progress in a relatively informal way. Our research indicates there is a merit in developing a "fitness for purpose" approach.[35] That is, instead of looking for joint working models which can be adopted "off the shelf", it is desirable to clarify overall purpose and stakeholder aims before selecting mechanisms.

Clearly there is a range of options which could develop from a "fitness for purpose" set of principles, and from these principles, choices for joint working arrangements emerge. Underlying the choices are the three routes to effective co-ordination identified in Chapter 2: hierarchy (involving an element of coercion); markets (involving trading of resources); and networks (involving working together around shared areas of agreement). In the four case studies examined in earlier chapters, all three driving forces can be seen to be at work.

In the sphere of community care, we have seen how central government can require co-ordination (and withhold funds if it is not forthcoming); how organisations trade resources and contract with each other to manage services; and how the development of shared beliefs around the philosophy of care in the community is critical.

In strategic planning, the exercise of hierarchical power appears to be less significant — although the local authorities recognise that, unless they get their act together, central government could step in to fill the vacuum. More important is the perception of mutual self-interest and shared understanding about the value of a strategic approach.

In corporate environmental policy making, our case study suggests hierarchical power is comparatively insignificant at the regional level. The joint working is driven by informal horizontal networks. These have been successful in fostering innovation and creating new links cross-cutting the public, private and voluntary sectors.

In transport planning, central government is able to exercise hierarchical power by imposing requirements relating to the allocation of transport supplementary grant — as with the All Wales Strategy approach to people with learning difficulties. Within this framework much, however, depends on local initiative and we have seen how different areas have adopted different strategies for bringing the different agencies together.

In some areas of policy making, central government may feel it has no alternative other than to force collaboration. In other areas it may feel a much more *laissez faire* approach will pay dividends. In the design of any inter-agency arrangement the purpose should remain the focus of attention. When this is clear, a variety of considerations in the architecture of joint working can then be addressed: formal/informal; member/officer; direct powers/advisory; continuous/time-limited; decisions on policy making/policy influencing; raising money/spending money; and so on. These are all key principles relating to the purpose of the organisation which should set the parameters for the design of inter-agency structures.

Our research shows that for many of the organisations there was a need to adapt and change but there was a problem in moving the basic model forward. In some cases the remit of the organisations had broadened — as for the strategic planning structures — but by and large the inter-agency arrangements studied have remained as created. This emphasises the need to choose a sound structure and working model at the beginning and to build one which is capable of modification.

One of the key issues in joint working is being clear about the constraints imposed both on the machinery itself and on the scope of the organisation. The constraints may not always be articulated but, in terms of accountability for decision making and expenditure, are there in reality. It may be sensible at the setting up of joint arrangements not only to state the objectives of the organisations but also the limits. The downside of this is that it can deter innovation and may not always be appropriate where ideas are still developing.

The influence of resources

The research suggests that availability of resources plays a critical role in inter-agency working. Put candidly, resources can spur collaboration into life — for example, transport and supplementary grant and Welsh Office funding for helping people with learning difficulties. In some cases, demonstrated collaboration is an essential prerequisite for financial allocation — for example, in City Challenge and in certain European Union programmes. In those joint working networks where resource allocation is not attached, there is less imperative to become directly involved. In the case of transport, the research clearly shows that many of the participants were drawn into the arrangements to acquire access to the grant. On this basis, the carrot of financial inducement is seen as vital in terms of keeping everyone on board.

It is essential to distinguish between the process of bidding for resources from those aspects of resourcing which allow the joint working machinery to take place. This, for many smaller authorities and agencies, is an immediate constraint. For local authorities under financial pressure, belonging to external organisations, particularly where there is no statutory requirement, can sometimes be viewed as a luxury. Resources were identified in the survey as being a clear constraint on the activity of some of the groupings. For example, the South West Regional Guidance had been produced from the small contributions of the membership.

As well as finding new funding, it is often hard to sustain existing voluntary joint arrangements where overall budgets in local authorities are constantly being cut. The ability to keep everyone "on board" is in constant danger,where total budgets are decreasing and the joint arrangement is discretionary rather than mandatory.

Managing cultural realignment

It is possible to view inter-agency arrangements as instruments for the management of change — not only change in policies and spending but also change in practice and approach. Inter-agency working often takes place in a framework of deep-seated value systems rooted in professional and/or organisational histories. In all the case studies, we became aware of what might best be described as clashes of culture between the various players. This may require the development of fresh understanding between these players and may necessitate a complete cultural realignment. This cultural realignment has to take place at both the political and officer level.

The experience with joint planning in the field of community care illustrates this argument well. Here, various professional battalions can be found competing to impose their definition of the agenda on their partners, or as some would see it, rivals. In the examination of the arrangement for helping people with learning difficulties in Avon, it was suggested that there was a huge communication gap between the relevant health trust and the county social services department. This can only be understood in the context of long-separated professional cultures being forced to come to terms with new attitudes and challenges, some of which question deeply-cherished beliefs. The idea of a joint commissioning team, entirely separate from the parent departments, is a bold initiative which is concerned to reshape attitudes as well as develop new policies.

The difference in cultures is often not openly acknowledged and, therefore, is not always addressed. It can be significant that it may be reflected in the culture of control. In many subject areas in joint working, for example in the environmental field, local authority contacts can see themselves as enablers/facilitators when in fact they are likely to remain firmly in control of both inter-agency structures and practical initiatives. Reference was made earlier to the way that central government may try to keep in control of the agenda and this can be problematic.

One way forward would be for the development of shared vision or values to be tackled at an early stage. The research shows that setting objectives was seen as crucial to the successful operation and outcome of joint working but this often did not spill over into considering values and vision. In some instances this may not be seen as of paramount importance but certainly, where there is a political component to the joint working, it may encourage differing attitudes to be addressed and accommodated.

As suggested in Chapter 2, effective joint working requires particular skills and the ability to network and communicate. This has implications for the training and development of all the people involved in inter-agency collaboration. From the examples looked at, this was generally not identified and certainly not prioritised. The overall approach was to address the "problem" rather than address wider issues of cultures, skills and visions. The more disparate the organisations involved, the more important it is for issues of shared values to be addressed. The research carried out for this report indicated that almost half the agencies involved were not local authorities. This is a significant comment on current inter-agency working in practice and indicates that there may be significant differences in culture from the local government norm.

Identification and ownership

This again is an issue for inter-agency working which may go unrecognised, certainly in the early stages of working. It may not be that important for inter-agency arrangements with a limited life, but for those which are expected to fulfil a function over a long period, there are interesting questions about who owns and identifies with the decisions made by inter-agency networks.

In terms of identity, the issue of giving everyone a stake, of creating an image and representation that is recognisable, can be important. In the case of environmental joint working, the designation of a physical space — the Cardiff Energy Centre and the CREATE Centre in Bristol — provides the immediate opportunity for identification. In the case of community care, a separate identity was established for the Avon Joint Health Commissioning Team, even to the extent of physically locating it in a separate building. Looking at the strategic planning examples, it would appear both are more nebulous as voluntary groupings with limited public profile. The identity largely does not spill out to its participants, with perhaps the exception of the authority that "hosts" the secretariat. Therefore, in reality, Gwent had become identified with the South Wales Standing Conference, and Somerset with the South West of England Conference.

For transport, there was a difference between the examples in that one was very much an on-the-ground inter-agency network with a clear service deliverer. For the Cardiff Region Public Transport Study, the issue of identity was not seen as too important. However, this project, which will need to have a long life if it is to move into implementation, has a key element of "ownership" built into it through multi-agency involvement. Therefore, the life and proposed impact of the organisation may very much depend on the ability of the arrangement to be identifiable and, in some sense, owned by the participating agencies.

There may be positive ways of securing this acceptance by using different forms of communication. The traditional local authority response of a committee report may not be the best vehicle. This rarely gets wider readership beyond the confines of the members on that committee. Newsletters, press releases and seminars are all approaches which keep people informed and "on board" and have been widely used by joint agencies.

In terms of officer working, the research showed a high degree of identification with the joint working by those officers involved. This was the case, perhaps surprisingly, where there was no secondment to joint teams but where officers were still based with their parent organisation. The problem for many of those officers is that the inter-agency work has little identity or sometimes significance in their own authority, which can present practical difficulties in allocating time or responsibility.

Innovation

Innovation is a feature of the inter-agency arrangements we have studied. For example, the environment case study uncovered innovation both in terms of the style of working among participants and in terms of encouraging innovation in the participants' home organisations. At local level, cultural innovation is well illustrated in the CREATE Centre in Bristol where city council officers now working alongside environmental groups have commented on ways in which their work style is changing.

The Welsh Environmental Co-ordinator's Forum has succeeded in spreading innovative policies and action from the most active local authorities to those which have previously been slow to develop a commitment in this non-statutory area. The forum is also innovatory as a vehicle for central/local government interaction. This is the only Wales-wide structure with which the Welsh

Office routinely engages which involves officers below chief officer level. For the officers responsible for environmental co-ordination, the forum has enhanced networking with other parts of central government. "Before this thing existed I would never have rung up [first name of Welsh Office representative] to find out the name of someone in the DoE."

Conclusion

The discussion of key themes in this section has highlighted not only the importance of developing improved horizontal links between agencies operating at local level but also the need to enhance vertical links between tiers of government. Central government can facilitate effective inter-agency working but it can also put sizeable obstacles in the way. The discussion has also suggested that a large number of developments are taking place in inter-agency working, a variety of approaches is possible and it is informative to juxtapose experience in different policy arenas.

While effective inter-agency working must depend on shared responsibility between agencies, the research suggests that local authorities can play a pivotal role. The evidence suggests local authorities are often orchestrating effective inter-agency working — a role which may go unrecognised. It is clear that, notwithstanding the examples of successful collaboration, there is a need for all agencies involved in joint working to think more deeply about their approach and ethos. Joint working can become a ritual dance in which partners shuffle uneasily around the floor. At its best, however, inter-agency collaboration can act as a powerful change driver generating new ideas, stimulating innovation and releasing new energies. By bringing agencies together, joint working can provoke questioning and reflection on the part of all involved. We conclude that, in a very important sense, inter-agency working can help organisations learn and change.

8. Summary and conclusions

At the beginning of this report, we suggested that changes in both the policy environment and the institutional environment are spurring local authorities into giving more attention to inter-agency working. Our research has suggested local authorities have a good deal of experience to draw on. In many ways it is quite wrong to describe them as monolithic service providers — local authorities have a track record of inter-agency collaboration stretching back over 20 years. Having said that, it does seem as if the need for improved approaches to inter-agency collaboration has grown in recent years, if only because of the fragmentation of the system of local governance.

To gain a better understanding of joint working, both between local authorities and between local authorities and other agencies, the Joseph Rowntree Foundation commissioned two research projects. The first study provides an examination of the joint arrangements for planning and managing services in the metropolitan areas of the country following the abolition of the metropolitan counties and the Greater London Council in 1986.[36] It concentrates on the formal inter-authority mechanisms set up to manage services required by statute. It examined joint boards, joint committees and agency arrangements, and concluded that, while services may be marginally less accountable and less accessible, they were not less effective. This second study has been designed to complement the first by examining experience in non-metropolitan areas, by studying informal as well as formal mechanisms for collaboration, and by including voluntary and private-sector organisations as well as public bodies within the research.

The previous section identifies the 11 major themes which have emerged from the research and there is no need to repeat them here. Rather, in this final section, we seek to provide a concise summary of our key findings structured under four headings:

1. The collaborative council
2. The performance of inter-agency collaboration
3. The future of inter-agency collaboration, and
4. Key lessons for policy.

The collaborative council

Legislative, financial, political and social changes are transforming the nature of local government. In many ways, notwithstanding the creation of unitary authorities in substantial parts of the country, the trend has been towards a diversification of the agencies delivering local services. Local authorities are questioning long-established organisational assumptions and a growing number now believe that, while direct provision may continue to be the best strategy for meeting local needs, there can be significant advantages in working with and through other agencies. In a wide range of areas, local authorities are now working more closely and effectively not just with other levels of government but also with other arms of government, with the voluntary sector and with the private sector.

To throw new light on these developments, this research has examined the collaborative council in action in four different policy settings:

● Community care — investigating joint planning between local authorities, health authorities, voluntary bodies and others to meet the needs of people with learning difficulties

● Strategic planning — assessing how local authorities collaborate at sub-regional and regional levels to prepare strategic land-use plans

● Environmental policy — evaluating ways in which local authorities, voluntary bodies and others are working together to pursue "greening" initiatives at local level

● Transport planning — examining how councils work with other agencies to prepare bids for transport supplementary grant.

These case studies have been chosen to illustrate a range of collaborative models (from formal through to very informal), a range of levels of decision making (from sub-regional strategy to specific projects in particular cities) and a range of policy areas (from land-use planning to social care). In each case study, the approach to inter-agency working in a geographical area in England is compared with an area in Wales.

At a conceptual level, the research has suggested that it is helpful to distinguish three approaches to the problems of public policy co-ordination. First, the power of **hierarchy** can be used to require, even coerce, co-operation between agencies. This approach may be necessary where a government is absolutely convinced that more voluntaristic arrangements will fail to secure collaboration. Thus, for example, the joint boards in the metropolitan areas seem to have been successful in delivering functions across local authority areas, albeit at the expense of local accountability.

A second approach uses the power of the **market** to achieve co-ordination through price signals which bring together demand and supply. This model, which uses contracting as a way of securing accountability and performance, seems to be particularly appropriate for services and activities which are relatively discrete and easily specified.

A third approach uses the power of **networks** to identify shared objectives, pool resources and achieve common purpose. The case studies examined in this report provide a picture of various kinds of networking in practice. Given our suggestion that the importance of developing improved approaches to boundary-spanning working is growing, it is hoped that the case studies will, in themselves, be useful to local authorities and agencies wanting to examine alternative models of collaboration. Often, debates about approaches to policy making and management take place in relatively sealed "policy communities". A strength of this report is that it juxtaposes experience from different policy settings and it is hoped this will stimulate fresh thinking.

The performance of inter-agency collaboration

The research has spelled out criteria for assessing inter-agency collaboration. There are two overarching requirements — **effective delivery** of function and adequate **accountability**. In joint working there can be a tension between these requirements. Much, however, depends on what the inter-agency collaboration is designed to achieve. Within the two broad categories, it is important to identify more specific criteria.

The **effectiveness** criterion concentrates on whether or not the arrangement is meeting its stated objectives. The four criteria of effectiveness used in this study are: objectives; value for money; responsiveness; and stability and flexibility.

The **accountability** criterion has gained prominence in recent years because of criticisms that the emerging systems of local governance can dilute, obscure and even erase the process of accountability. The three criteria of accountability used in this study are: relating to the public; political accountability; and financial accountability.

In addition to these criteria, which we hope authorities and agencies may find useful in appraising their own approach to inter-agency collaboration, the research has suggested that other cross-cutting factors can be enormously important. For example, the degree to which participants identify with a given arrangement can be crucial. Also the research has shown that inter-agency working can play an important role in staff development, organisational learning and the promotion of innovation. It follows that it is dangerous to generalise too freely about alternative models of collaboration. So much depends on local needs, political aspirations and citizen concerns. The research does, however, enable us to draw out some insights on the possible trajectory of inter-agency working in the future as well as identify some general lessons for policy.

The future of inter-agency collaboration

There is every reason to anticipate that the kind of collaboration and joint working which has become established in Britain in recent years will continue to develop and diversify in the future. An important underlying reason for this will be the continued pressure on resources and the fact that joint working, as can be seen from this study, is perceived to give both better value for money and added value. Similarly, the opportunities for bringing together different authors and styles of governance may give further impetus to develop and extend forms of collaboration. The trend towards partnership working in bidding for finance, developing policy and providing services has brought together varying cultures, and the research has shown that this is recognised by most participants as being a positive opportunity rather than a constraint.

On the negative side, the future is bringing another round of local government reorganisation which was perceived by all those affected to be a destabilising influence on joint working systems. From the survey carried out, continuity and stability were seen as important in terms of the confidence in collaboration and the ability to deliver. It may well be that local government reorganisation in the long run will give new openings for joint working. But in the short term it is often seen as a major concern and indeed a threat to some of the voluntary arrangements. It may well be that, as experience of these arrangements has shown, certain individuals or authorities take the lead and act as a catalyst for creating or extending a network.

In addition, looking to the future, further fragmentation of decision making/service delivery may reach a point where it undermines joint working and collaboration. Although in the past we have seen a great proliferation of agencies involved in local governance and this, in itself, has been a spur for collaboration, it may be that continued fragmentation may produce unmanageable numbers with smaller budgets. In such instances careful thought will need to be given to the management, in terms of both structures and processes, to keep everyone on board — particularly as the research emphasised that full participation by all contributors is a key factor in making collaboration work.

It should be noted as well that the current emphasis on the contract culture and service agreements in the public sector can have an inhibiting effect on joint working. The research clearly shows that a flexibility of approach, particularly where there are different cultures coming together, is often critical to developing joint working. This may be a vital factor limiting the involvement of some agencies and individuals where freedom to operate outside a contract specification does not exist.

Key lessons

This study has brought forward lessons for particular sectors in Chapters 3 to 6.

1) Recognition
Joint working is now an intrinsic part of local governance. The collaborative council is very much the picture of local government today and this is likely to continue into the future. The presence and value of this joint working needs to be recognised. Joint working should not be seen as either an "add on" or peripheral — it needs to be taken seriously at both the political and professional technical levels. Joint working needs to be accounted for, where appropriate, in terms of job descriptions, skills, training and resources, and responsibility needs to be more clearly defined and respected.

2) Getting the right model
There is a whole range of collaborative activities: some of which have been clearly thought out at the beginning and others which have grown in an organic way. It is important that the vehicle of collaboration is fit for the purpose intended. This will require budgets, objectives, roles, structures and processes to be clearly defined; occasionally it will require joint arrangements to be time limited. All of this will require clear definition and clarity of purpose. Traditional forms of local-authority-centred arrangements may not always be the best model when there is a need to draw together a diverse range of cultures.

3) Achieving accountability
Mechanisms and routes of accountability appear to be more obscure and diffuse in joint working arrangements than through a traditional single local council. This needs to be thought about at an early stage with perhaps new methods of communications being tried. Above all, political responsibilities need to be thought out so that elected representatives can have a clear and useful role in collaboration.

4) Review mechanisms
Because many joint arrangements take place outside the council, they may go unrecognised and can have an indeterminate life of their own. These arrangements need to have a clear internal reporting mechanism, and they need to be drawn into a policy and performance review system which allows monitoring against their objectives. This process, above all others, may be the critical lesson to be learned from the exercise, and would allow joint working and collaboration to be a legitimate and mainstream activity.

References

1) Roberts V., Russell H., Harding A. and Parkinson M. (1995) *Public/private/voluntary partnerships in local government*, Local Government Management Board, Luton; Bailey N. (1995) *Partnership agencies in British urban policy*, UCL Press, London.

2) Smith R., Gaster L., Harrison L., Martin L., Means R. and Thistlethwaite P. (1993) *Working together for better community care*, School for Advanced Urban Studies, University of Bristol; Nocon A. (1994) *Collaboration in community care in the 1990s*, Business Education Publishers Ltd., Sunderland.

3) Local Government Management Board (1993) *A framework for local sustainability*, Local Government Management Board, Luton; Commission of the European Communities (1992) *Towards sustainability: A European Community programme of policy action in relation to the environment and sustainable development*. COMM (92) 23 Brussels.

4) Clarke M. (1994) *The new local governance*, European Policy Forum, London, p1.

5) Osborne D. and Gaebler T. (1993) *Reinventing government. How the entrepreneurial spirit is transforming the public sector*, Plume, New York.

6) Hambleton R. and Essex S. (1994) *Working across organisational boundaries: Learning from the Welsh experience*, Local Government Management Board, Luton.

7) Working Party Report (1993) *Fitness for purpose. Shaping new patterns of organisation and management*, Local Government Management Board, Luton, p11.

8) Travers T., Biggs S. and Jones G. (1995) *Joint working between local authorities. Experience from the metropolitan areas*, Joseph Rowntree Foundation, LGC Communications, London.

9) Webb A. (1991) Co-ordination: a problem in public sector management, *Policy and Politics*, Vol 19, No 4, pp229-241.

10) Working Party op cit, pp43-44.

11) Thompson G., Frances J., Levacic R., and Mitchell J. (1991) *Markets, hierarchies and networks. The co-ordination of social life*, Sage Publications, London.

12) Ibid, p14.

13) This is not a new idea. See, for example, Schon D.A. (1971) *Beyond the stable state*. Temple Smith, London, p200.

14) Travers T. et al, op cit, p9.

15) *Commission for Local Democracy (1995) Taking charge: the rebirth of local democracy*, Municipal Journal Books, London.

16) Leach S. (1994) The unkillable tier, *Local Government Chronicle*, 1 July, p18.

17) Association of District Councils (1993) *Towards unitary authorities: joint arrangements*, A paper from the series of Local Government Review Advice Papers for District Councils, Association of District Councils, London.

18) Welsh Office (1983) *All Wales strategy for development of services for mentally handicapped people*, Welsh Office, Cardiff.

19) Department of Health (1989) *Caring for people: community care in the next decade and beyond*. Cm 849, HMSO, London.

20) Welsh Office (1992) *The All Wales mental handicap strategy*. Framework for development from April 1993, Welsh Office, Cardiff.

21) This history is documented in: Means R. and Smith R. (1994) *Community care. Policy and practice*, London: Macmillan; Malin N. (ed) (1994) *Implementing community care*, Open University Press, Buckingham; Nocon A. op cit.

22) Griffiths R. (1988) *Community care: agenda for action*. London: HMSO.

23) Crowson D. (1991) *A job half done*. Mencap in Wales, Cardiff.

24) Mapp S. (1995) Joint effort, *Community Care*, 11-17 May, pp16-17.

25) Standing Conference on Regional Policy in South Wales, (1994) *South Wales Renewable Energy Study*, Planning Policy Guidelines.

26) Department of Environment and Welsh Office (1993) *Renewable Energy*, Planning Brief Guidance Note 22.

27) Department of the Environment (1994) *Regional Planning Guidance for South West England*.

28) Association of Metropolitan Authorities, (1995) *Regionalism: the local government dimension*, Association of Metropolitan Authorities, London.

29) Ibid.

30) Local Government Management Board, op cit; Blowers A. (ed) (1993) *Planning for a sustainable environment*. A report by the Town and Country Planning Association, London.

31) Department of the Environment (1992) *Development plans and regional planning guidance*, Planning Policy Guidance note 12, London.

32) Department of the Environment (1994) Transport Planning Policy Guidance note 13, London.

33) Royal Commission on Environmental Pollution (1994) *Transport and the environment*, Eighteenth Report, Cm 2674, HMSO, London.

34) Leach S. et al (1992) *After abolition: the operation of the post-1986 metropolitan government system in England*, Institute of Local Government Studies, Birmingham.

35) We draw this idea from the Local Government Management Report guidance document on internal management — see Working Party Report, op cit. This argues that local authority management arrangements should be fit for the purpose intended. The same approach should be applied to inter-agency working.

36) Travers T. et al, op cit.